Storybook
Favourites
in
Cross-stitch

Storybook Favourites in Cross-stitch

Gillian Souter

LITTLE, BROWN AND COMPANY
Boston New York Toronto London

A LITTLE, BROWN BOOK

First published in hardback in Great Britain 1995
by Little, Brown and Company (UK)
Reprinted 1995, 1996
This paperback edition first published in 1998

Created and designed by Off the Shelf Publishing,
32 Thomas Street, Lewisham, NSW 2049, Australia

Copyright © Off the Shelf Publishing, 1995, 1998
The moral right of the author has been asserted.

A CIP catalogue record for this book
is available from the British Library

ISBN 0-316-64435-8

10 9 8 7 6 5 4 3 2 1

Colour reproduction by Kyodo Printing
Produced by Phoenix Offset
Printed and bound in China

Little, Brown and Company (UK)
Brettenham House
Lancaster Place
London WC2E 7EN

Contents

Introduction

This book is filled with ideas—some simple and some more elaborate—for children's gifts in cross-stitch. So that you're not the only one who gets enjoyment out of the process, all the designs are based on favourite characters from children's books. Some of them—Peter Rabbit, Paddington, Rupert— were my companions as I grew up. Others, such as Spot, Duck and Angelina, are ones I've grown fond of in my second childhood. Styles of illustration differ greatly and this is reflected in the designs. Beatrix Potter's delicate watercolours need to be rendered in pastel shades and an impressionistic style. Stitching Bruna's boldly drawn characters is more like colouring in, although you don't see the final effect until the backstitching is added. As the aim was to represent the original illustrations as faithfully as possible, most of the designs are stitched on white backgrounds and use quite a lot of half-stitch (or three-quarter stitch as it is sometimes called). For those who are new to cross-stitch, the Apple Tree Farm letters, which contain no half-stitches, are a good starting point. Each design is made into a finished project: these are merely suggestions and there are countless ways of showcasing each design.

Basic Techniques

Cross-stitch is one of the most popular of crafts and is extremely simple to learn. If you are new to this form of embroidery, this chapter will give you all the information you need to complete the projects in this book.

In cross-stitch, a pattern is transferred from a charted design to a piece of un-marked fabric. The chart is a grid of squares with symbols forming the design. A key tells you which colour of embroidery thread relates to which symbol on the chart. Working the design is simply a matter of stitching a series of crosses in the appropriate colour according to the arrangement on the chart.

Types of Fabric

The fabric used for cross-stitch must be of an evenweave, that is, have the same number of threads over a given distance both vertically and horizontally. Many types of fabric are suitable for cross-stitch, but either embroidery linen or Aida is ideal. Linen is woven in single threads; Aida has even bands or groups of threads.

The size of each stitch is determined by the number of fabric threads over which you sew and by the number of bands or threads per inch of fabric (known as the fabric count). Most fabric counts are still given in inches, even in countries which have adopted the metric system. Linen 26 has twenty-six threads per inch of fabric and

each stitch covers two threads (to prevent the embroidery thread gliding under a fabric thread) so there are thirteen stitches per inch. With Linen 30, there are fifteen stitches per inch: the larger the fabric count, the smaller the stitches will be.

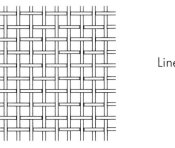

Linen

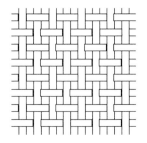

Aida

Estimating Size

The instructions for each project specify the type of fabric used to stitch it and the amount of fabric required. When you choose a fabric with a different thread count, you will need to calculate what the size of the stitched design will be. Use the following rule: finished size equals the design stitch count divided by the fabric thread count.

When using linen, you stitch over two threads. Therefore, a stitch count of 50 x 50 (i.e. 50 squares on the chart each way) must be divided by 13, if using Linen 26, or by 15 (Linen 30) and so on. Aida also comes in various counts: if using Aida 14, divide the stitch count by 14. Multiply the result by 2.5 to convert from inches into centimetres.

Preparing the Fabric

To prevent the fabric from fraying, zigzag the edges on a sewing machine or simply use masking tape which can later be removed.

Locate the centre of the fabric by folding it in half and then in half again. If you are working on a large design, mark the centre with a pin and use a coloured thread to tack from side to side and from top to bottom, each time tacking through the centre mark. This should quarter your fabric. When you start cross-stitching, make sure the centre of the design (indicated by arrows on the chart) matches the centre point of your fabric.

Embroidery Thread

Cross-stitch is generally worked in stranded cotton embroidery thread. The designs in this book have all been stitched using DMC stranded cotton. If you wish to use a different brand, match the colours shown in the pictures as closely as possible or choose your own combinations.

The key for each design lists: a symbol which appears in the chart, a corresponding DMC thread number, a colour name for easy identification, and the number of stitches to be made in that colour. It is impossible to gauge the exact amount of thread needed

but this will give an idea of the relative quantities required for each colour. As a very rough guide, a block of 100 cross-stitches on Aida 14 requires 50 cm of embroidery thread using two strands at a time.

The six strands of the embroidery thread can be split into single strands, three lengths of double strands, or other combinations. The number of strands used depends on the count of your fabric. In general, using more strands will make your finished work more vivid, but if you use too many strands they will not fit neatly within the weave of the fabric. Below is a suggested number of strands for different fabric counts. It is a good idea, though, to add an extra strand when stitching the design on a dark fabric.

Count	Cross-stitch strands	Backstitch strands
Aida 11	3	2
Aida 14	2	1
Aida 18	2	1
Aida 22	1	1
Linen 16	3	2
Linen 20	2	1
Linen 26	2	1
Linen 32	1	1

Equipment

Use a blunt needle such as a small tapestry needle that will not split the fabric threads. Match the size of the needle to the size of the hole: a size 24 needle is suitable for Linen 20 or Aida 11 whereas a size 26 needle would be appropriate for Aida 14.

You will need two pairs of scissors: a small pair for trimming threads and a pair of shears for cutting the fabric.

If you are stitching one of the larger designs, or any that require several similar shades of embroidery thread, your spare strands can easily become jumbled. To make a simple thread holder like the one pictured, cut a length of sturdy card and use a hole punch to cut holes at regular intervals. Mark the colour number and the appropriate symbol alongside the hole and tie your threads as shown.

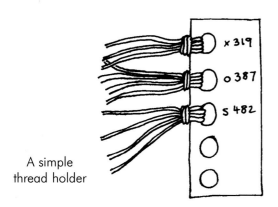

A simple
thread holder

A frame or embroidery hoop will help you to stitch evenly and prevent warping, but it is not necessary for very small designs. Choose a hoop which will fit the whole design, otherwise it will damage existing stitches.

Reading the Charts

Each square on the chart represents a full cross-stitch and each symbol represents a colour as specified in the key. A heavy line indicates where to backstitch and the key will tell you which colour to use for each section of backstitching. Arrows indicate the centre of the design.

Check the instructions regarding the position of the stitching on the fabric; if there are no specific instructions, orient the fabric to match the chart and stitch the design in the centre. Find the colour represented by the centre symbol and start on that block of colour.

Cut a 50 cm length of embroidery thread and gently split it into the appropriate number of strands. Let the strands dangle and untwist.

Cross-stitching

Thread the needle with the appropriate number of strands and bring it through the fabric, leaving 2 cm of waste thread at the back. Hold this tail carefully and make sure that your first four or five stitches secure it. Then trim any excess.

Stitch a series of diagonal bars running from left to right. Then, at the end of the row, return by stitching the top bars from right to left. Drop your needle to the bottom of the next row and repeat the process. Stitches in a sequence interlock, sharing holes with the neighbouring stitch.

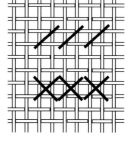

Forming cross-stitches
on linen

Forming cross-stitches
on Aida

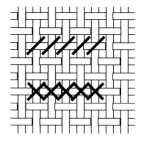

Remember, the number of threads crossed by a single stitch will depend on your fabric: on linen, each stitch covers two threads, on Aida each stitch covers one band of threads. This is shown more clearly in the two diagrams on page 10.

Always work horizontally rather than vertically and do not change directions; even though you may use more embroidery thread the result will look much neater.

Once you have stitched some crosses, use them as your reference point and count from them, rather than from the centre. Your tacked centre lines remain useful as a cross-check that you are counting correctly. Complete each block of colour, jumping short distances where necessary, but always securing the thread at the back by running the needle under existing threads. If blocks are some distance apart, finish off the first and start afresh.

To finish off each section, run your needle through the back of four or five stitches and trim the embroidery thread close to the cloth.

Half-stitch

Many of the charts contain some half-stitches or, as they are sometimes called, three-quarter stitches. These are indicated on the chart by a right-angled triangle and are usually found around the edges of a design. In this case, one diagonal of the cross-stitch is formed in the usual way, but the second stitch is brought down into the central hole of linen, or into the centre of an Aida block.

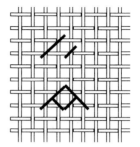

Forming two half-stitches

Where the chart indicates two half-stitches in the same square, you will need to decide which colour should predominate in the second diagonal.

Backstitch

Many of the charts include backstitching to define outlines and provide detail. It is indicated by a solid line on the chart. Backstitch is always worked after cross-stitching is completed and is worked in a continuous line. The method is best described in the diagram below.

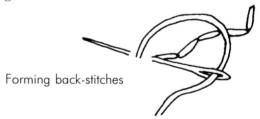

Forming back-stitches

Some Tips

It is important to keep your work as clean and fresh as possible. Don't leave unfinished work in an embroidery hoop for too long as the hoop may mark the fabric. When not in use, always secure the needle at the edge of the fabric to prevent rust marks or thread distortion from spoiling your stitching.

Do not fold work-in-progress; roll it in a layer of tissue paper. A sheet of acetate (available from art supply shops) offers good protection for a large project.

Cut your embroidery thread, as you need it, into 50 cm lengths. Longer strands will start to fray towards the end.

After working a series of stitches, your thread will start to twist. This can give uneven stitches, so occasionally let the needle dangle down from the fabric so that the thread can unwind.

When moving from one area of a colour to another patch of the same colour, don't jump the thread across the back if the gap will remain bare. Such leaps will show through the fabric in the finished work.

If you make an error in counting, do not try to rescue the embroidery thread for reuse. Use a pair of small pointed scissors to snip misplaced stitches and carefully pull out the strands, then stitch correctly with a new piece of embroidery thread.

Avoid the temptation to start or finish off with a knot; it will form a lump when the work is laid flat.

Teaching Children

There was a time when every child, or at least every girl, was expected to cross-stitch a sampler. As it was usually a prescribed design of letters and numbers with little or no decoration, it must have seemed more of a chore than a pleasure.

The designs in this book will no doubt tempt many boys and girls to take up the craft of cross-stitch and it is important to start them on simple and achievable projects which will not dampen their enthusiasm and deter their interest.

Here are some tips:

- Encourage children to practise the basic cross-stitch by creating coloured patterns on scrap fabric before tackling a design.

- Explain how the key works, making sure they understand that each symbol represents a particular colour.

- Children may like to colour in the key and the chart (you may photocopy a design from the book provided it is for personal use only).

- Choose a large count Aida fabric and a large blunt needle for them to work with.

- Choose a small design which has big blocks of solid colour. Introduce half-stitches only once they have mastered the full cross-stitch. The letter designs for *Apple Tree Farm* have no half-stitches and one of these may be a good starting point.

- Supervise backstitching to begin with. It may be appropriate for you to work the backstitch for younger children.

- Help children make their stitched design into a finished project that they can use or display.

- Help children to chart their own initials, name, or age, using the alphabet and number charts on pages 124-5. If they stitch their name and age on a design, it both personalises it and becomes a milestone in a child's life.

In the Nursery

The birth of a baby
is a special event and is worth
marking with a handmade gift.
This section includes an array of
wonderful ideas, many of which
will no doubt become treasured
heirlooms. Peter Rabbit adds a
lovely touch to a nursery deco-
rated in pastels, while Blinky Bill
and Babar will brighten the room.
You can also use other designs
from the book to adorn such useful things as a crib sheet, a quilt,
or a travel bag to hold all those
baby necessities.

Blinky Bill

For some sixty years, Australian children have delighted in the antics of a mischievous koala with a penchant for baggy checked trousers. Blinky Bill first appeared in 1933 and was the creation of Dorothy Wall who had emigrated to Australia after studying art in New Zealand. Her first story, simply named Blinky Bill, was quickly followed by Blinky Bill Grows Up and then by Blinky Bill and Nutsy; all three stories were then reprinted together as The Complete Adventures of Blinky Bill. Blinky, who usually sports a slingshot (and is often in trouble as a result), has a curious nature and is intrigued by his fellow bush creatures and by humans that he encounters. The popularity of the cheeky koala was such that the publishers continued to produce books about him after Dorothy Wall's death in 1942. He has since appeared on postage stamps, in advertising campaigns and, most recently, as the star of an animated film.

Welcome Cards

These cheeky designs of Blinky Bill and his girlfriend Nutsy can be stitched quite quickly to welcome a baby girl or boy.

Materials: 20 x 15 cm cream Aida fabric with 11 thread groups per inch; pale card; double-sided tape; DMC embroidery threads listed.

Stitch count: 46H x 25W - Nutsy
46H x 37W - Blinky

Directions: Stitch a character on fabric and press. Cut 16 x 39 cm of card and score it with a knife to create three equal panels. Trim a narrow strip off the left panel. Cut a window in the centre panel to fit the design. Stick double-sided tape on the inside of the centre panel, position the embroidery and stick down the left-hand panel as a backing.

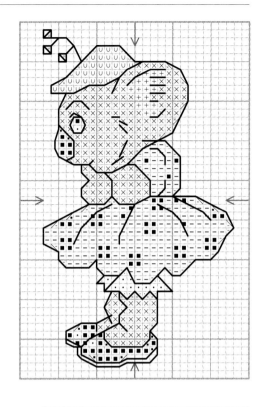

KEY for Nutsy

	DMC	Colour	Stitches
+	300	dark brown	18
■	310	black	83
U	321	crimson	42
−	743	gold	187
×	922	orange	229
•		white	25
	310	black	backstitch

KEY for Blinky Bill

	DMC	Colour	Stitches
+	300	dark brown	127
■	310	black	84
U	353	pink	8
×	922	orange	602
O	3760	blue	293
•		white	31
	310	black	backstitch

Make a special card for a very
special occasion. Instructions can
be found on page 17.

Blinky Bill © Angus & Robertson Publishers, 1939.

*Start a child off on their journey
with this delightful picture of
Blinky Bill. The chart appears
on page 20.*

Framed Picture

This classic illustration of Blinky Bill off on his adventures, complete with slingshot, billy can and swag, makes a delightful framed picture to decorate a nursery.

Materials: 40 x 40 cm of cream Aida fabric with 14 thread groups per inch; DMC embroidery threads listed.

Stitch count: 82H x 95W

Directions: Stitch the design in the centre of the Aida fabric. Press the work carefully and have it professionally framed.

	KEY for Blinky setting out		
	DMC	Colour	Stitches
■	310	black	597
−	414	dark grey	119
N	606	red	569
T	610	dark brown	89
\	611	brown	688
o	612	light brown	678
+	613	sand	251
✳	647	grey	78
↑	648	light grey	60
·	676	light gold	194
▲	680	gold brown	99
=	729	gold	196
⌐	840	dark fawn	310
●	898	chocolate	119
✕	972	yellow	551
U	3772	liver	258
<		white	27

Backstitch

	white	shoes
310	black	eyes, nose, mouth, tin, slingshot, suit
898	brown	other details

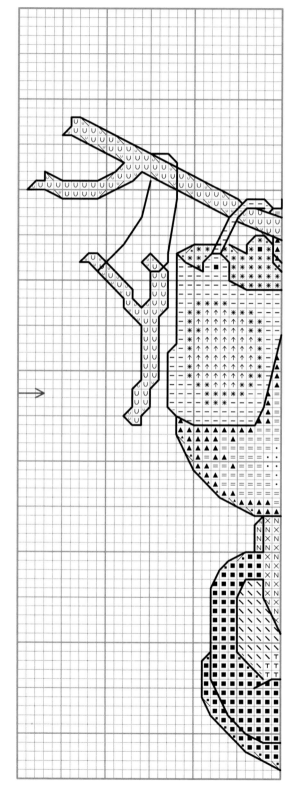

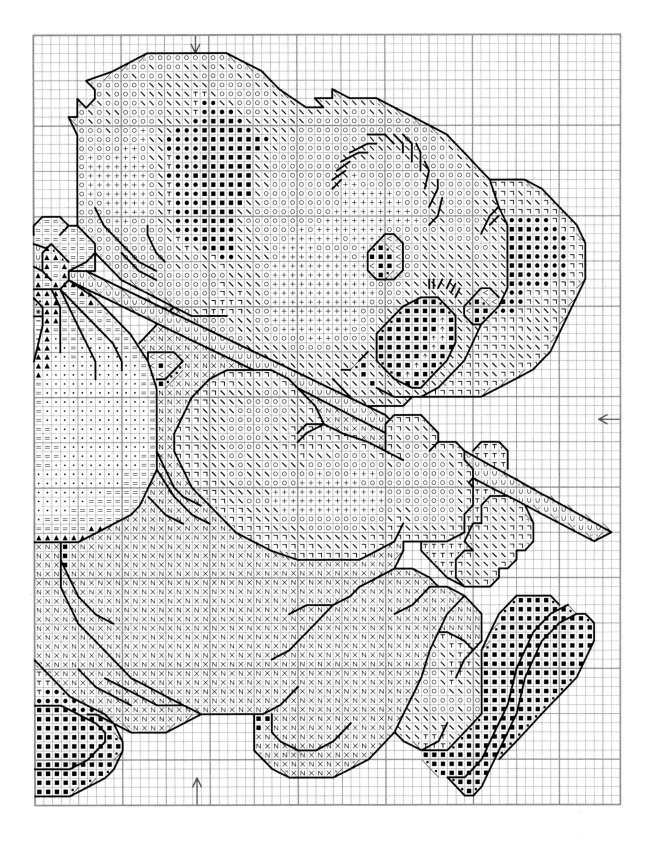

Clare
Cavanagh
born
21.6.93

THE TAILOR OF GLOUCESTER

THE TAILOR OF GLOUCESTER

THE TALE OF TOM KITTEN

THE TALE OF BENJAMIN BUNNY

THE TALE OF SAMUEL WHISKERS

BEATRIX POTTER

Peter Rabbit

This most famous of rabbits first appeared in an illustrated letter written by Beatrix Potter to cheer up a little boy who was ill in bed. Beatrix's own childhood had been a rather lonely one and on September 4th 1893, she wrote "My dear Noel, I don't know what to write to you, so I shall tell you a story." In the following eight pages, she told the story that was to become the most popular children's book of all time—The Tale of Peter Rabbit. It was some years before Beatrix could find a publisher for her story, but once it appeared in 1902, it was a great commercial success and she went on to create many more books suitable for small hands. The characters, including Benjamin Bunny, Jemima Puddleduck, Mrs Tiggy-winkle, were based on real creatures: pets and wildlife found in the Lake District where Beatrix spent her holidays and later chose to live. The accuracy of her paintings and the gentle humour in her text ensured the lasting success of Beatrix Potter's books, which have been published in many languages and are still enjoyed by children and parents alike.

Birth Announcement

Many of Beatrix Potter's best loved characters are woven into this beautiful birth announcement. Most of the work can be done while waiting for the baby's arrival.

Materials: 45 x 40 cm of white linen
             with 11 threads per centimetre;
             DMC embroidery threads listed.

Stitch count: 180H x 153W

Directions: Tack marking lines to divide the fabric into four (see page 9) and stitch the characters and the backstitching. Use the alphabet and number charts on pages 124-5 to chart the baby's name and date of birth on graph paper. Cross-stitch these in position. Press the completed work carefully and have it professionally framed.

	DMC	Colour	Stitches		DMC	Colour	Stitches
X	353	peach	675	—	775	pale blue	218
*	413	charcoal	12	+	794	blue	257
S	414	light grey	68	I	841	fawn	371
I	437	tan	206	\	842	light fawn	99
▼	471	dark green	34	▲	932	grey-blue	121
O	472	green	318	‖	976	very dark tan	81
F	504	mint	174	T	977	dark tan	186
U	543	flesh	127	↑	3689	pink	132
●	640	brown	60	L	3713	pale pink	181
4	642	light brown	138	•		white	268
=	644	sand	70				
>	712	cream	164				
N	738	light tan	296				
<	760	rose	146				

KEY for Beatrix Potter sampler

Backstitch

310	black	hedgehog
794	blue	tendrils
413	charcoal	other details

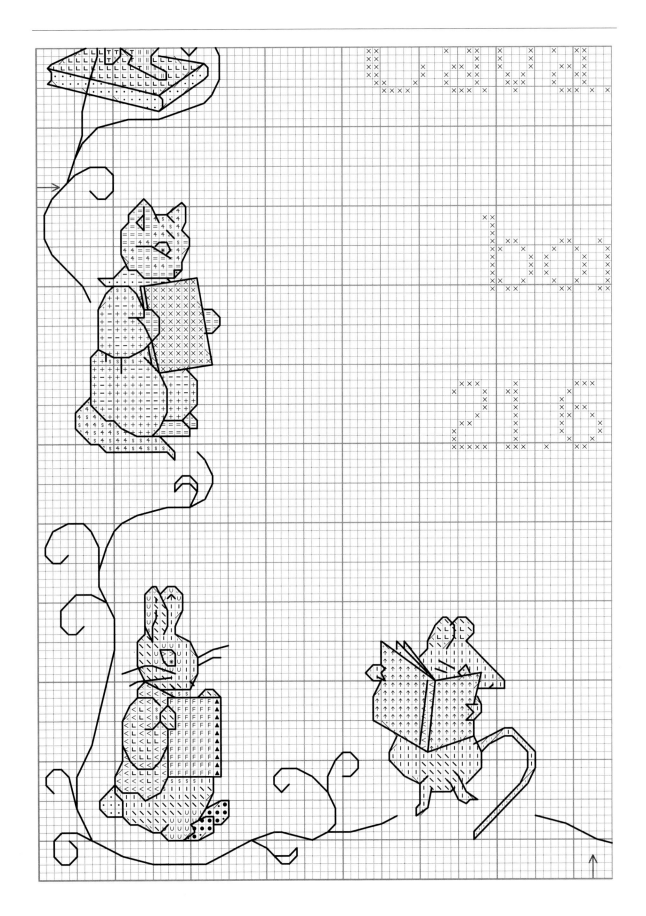

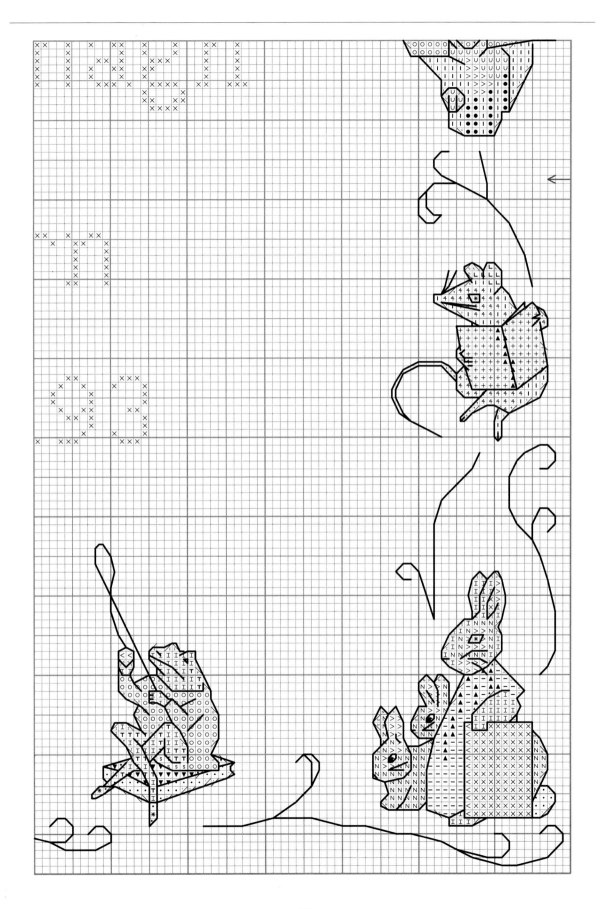

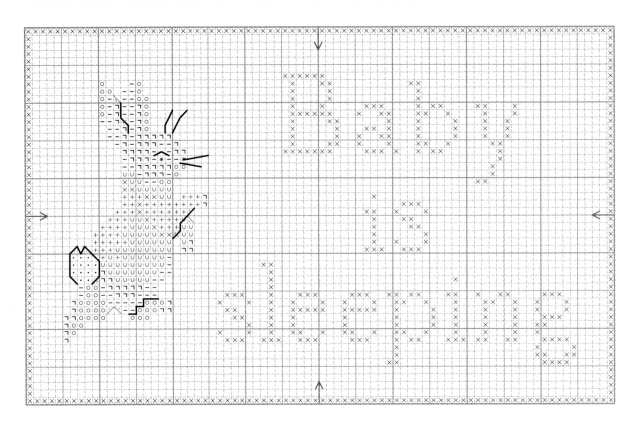

Sleep Notice

Peter Rabbit, in his classic pose, guards the door of a sleeping child. As an option, you could replace 'baby' with a name.

Materials: 30 x 25 cm of white Aida fabric
with 11 thread groups per inch;
40 cm ribbon;
22 x 16 cm felt;
21 x 15 cm heavy white card;
DMC embroidery threads listed.

Stitch count: 50H x 80W

Directions: Stitch the design, inserting a child's name if desired (see pages 124-5). Carefully press the work. Cut a 21 x 15 cm piece of white card. Centre the embroidered work over the card, fold the edges over and glue them onto the back of the card, so that

the work is taut. Cut a 40 cm length of ribbon and glue the ends at the back of the top right and left corners. Cut a 22 x 16 cm rectangle of felt and glue it to cover the back of the notice. The felt should extend evenly around all edges as a border.

	KEY for Peter Rabbit		
	DMC	*Colour*	*Stitches*
∗	413	grey	2
⅂	437	dark tan	64
−	738	tan	64
O	739	light tan	48
X	798	dark blue	535
U	809	blue	71
+	3747	pale blue	54
•		white	18
	413	grey	backstitch

Pin Holder

Mrs Tiggy-winkle, the hedgehog who takes in the animals' washing, seems an ideal decoration for this safety pin holder.

Materials: 20 x 20 cm of white linen with 11 threads per centimetre; 20 x 20 cm coloured fabric; polyester toy stuffing; DMC embroidery threads listed.

Stitch count: 52H x 52W

Directions: Stitch the design in the centre of the fabric and carefully press the finished work. Zigzag the edges of both the linen and the backing fabric. Place the two pieces together with right sides facing and sew them together, leaving a gap of several centimetres along one edge. Turn the pillow inside out so that the design faces out and fill it with the polyester stuffing. Neatly handsew the opening closed. Attach safety pins for a useful gift.

	DMC	Colour	Stitches
■	310	black	3
Z	318	light grey	89
X	434	brown	248
>	436	light brown	267
U	472	green	115
●	601	dark pink	30
–	603	pink	54
○	605	light pink	80
＼	793	blue	115
▲	801	dark brown	95
↑	3747	light blue	85
+		ecru	52
=		white	308

KEY for Mrs Tiggy-winkle

Backstitch
310	black	face, cloth
801	dark brown	spines
317	dark grey	other

Right: This cushion for safely holding nappy pins features Mrs Tiggy-winkle; see page 29. Instructions for the lidded box can be found on page 32.

Below: Peter Rabbit offers a gentle warning not to disturb. The pattern appears on page 28, along with instructions for making the sign.

Lidded Box

This fabric-covered box is ideal for holding cotton balls or nappy pins. The lid features Mrs Rabbit dosing a slightly ill but very naughty Peter with camomile tea.

Materials: 15 x 15 cm of white Aida fabric with 14 thread groups per inch; thin wadding; card; coloured fabric; DMC embroidery threads listed.

Stitch count: 56H x 56W

Directions: Stitch the design on the Aida fabric and press the finished work. Trim this into a circle, allowing 1 cm around the stitched border.

Cut a strip 4 cm wide and 40 cm long on the diagonal of the coloured fabric, creating a bias strip. Position the strip face down on the stitched design and sew the edges, allowing a 5 mm seam. Zigzag edges to secure.

Use a compass to draw five circles on card: one with a 6 cm radius, two with a 5.5 cm radius and two with a 5 cm radius. Cut out each disc and attach a layer of wadding to the largest one with dabs of glue. Place the Aida over the wadding and glue the raw edge of the bias strip on the back of the card.

Cover one of the 5.5 cm radius discs as a base. Cut a piece of card 40 x 6 cm and glue the short ends to form a cylinder to fit the covered base. Cut a 42 x 8 cm strip of fabric and glue it around the cylinder. Snip darts in the fabric overlapping the base and glue them down. Cut a 35 x 5 cm piece of card and cover one side with fabric, gluing down each edge at the back. Glue this piece around the inside of the box, as a lining.

Cover the two smaller discs and glue one onto the underneath of the lid and the other inside the box. Cover the last disc and glue it onto the outside base of the box, covering the tabs.

KEY for Mrs Rabbit & Peter			
	DMC	Colour	Stitches
X	353	apricot	185
T	414	grey	2
Z	437	tan	25
∩	738	light tan	62
+	739	cream	186
U	772	pale green	102
▲	813	blue	83
/	818	pink	161
O	827	pale blue	127
✳	928	ice	55
N	954	green	31
•		white	448
	414	grey	backstitch

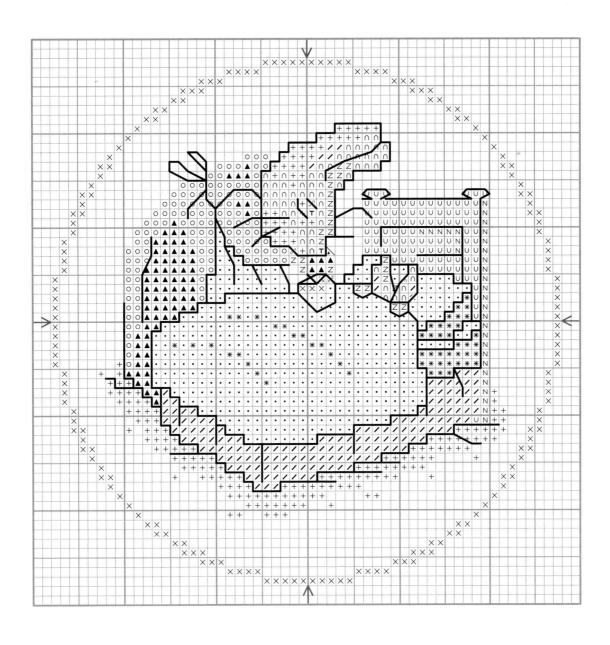

Babar

Over sixty years ago, a Parisian mother made up a lively bedtime story about a young elephant who grows up to become a wise and much-loved king. Cecile de Brunhoff's sons were so enchanted by the tale that they recounted it to their artist father Jean and persuaded him to illustrate it. The adventures of Babar, who was given a dashing green jacket and red bow tie, were produced in book form through the good grace of two uncles in the publishing industry and a classic of children's literature was born. Jean de Brunhoff wrote and illustrated another eleven Babar books before his death from tuberculosis. After such a family effort, it was a natural conclusion that Laurent, the eldest of those children to hear the bedtime story, should continue the tradition. The many books have since been translated from French into twelve languages and an animated version is winning Babar new friends around the world.

Soft Toys

Bright, solid colours soon catch a baby's eye and these delightful Babar and Celeste toys will make great cot companions.

Materials: 25 x 20 cm of white Aida fabric with 11 thread groups per inch; 25 x 20 cm of backing fabric; polyester toy stuffing; DMC embroidery threads listed.

Stitch count: 62H x 51W - Babar
63H x 41W - Celeste

Directions: Stitch the design on the Aida fabric and carefully press the finished work. Trim around the design, allowing a 2 cm margin, and zigzag to secure edges. Trim and zigzag backing fabric to match. Lay the two together with right sides facing and sew around the design, allowing a 1 cm seam, and leaving a gap of several centimetres.

Turn the toy right side out and fill it with polyester stuffing. Handsew the gap closed, making sure no stuffing can be pulled out.

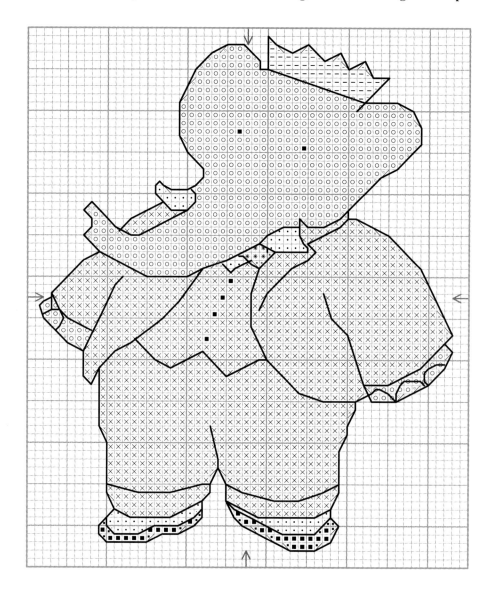

KEY for Babar and Celeste		
DMC	Colour	Stitches
■ 310	black	51
✳ 350	rose	8
○ 453	grey	1288
✕ 702	green	1178
+ 892	pink	1159
− 972	yellow	99
•	white	120
310	black	backstitch

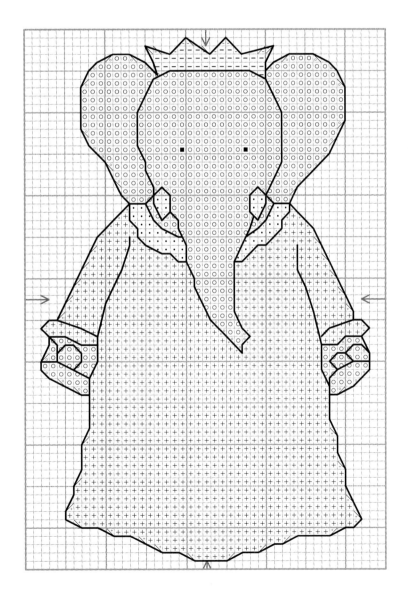

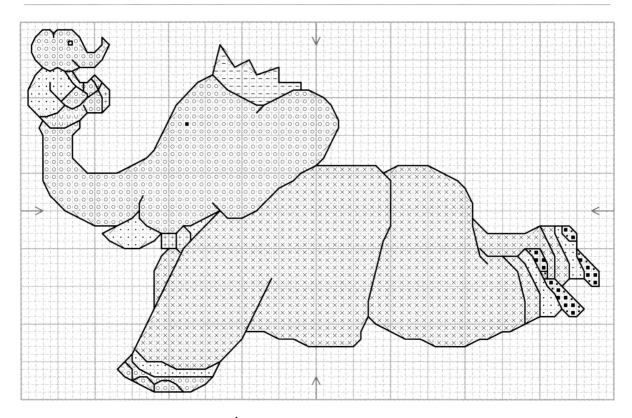

Bath Wrap

Keep baby snug after a bath with this elegant bath wrap. The hood features Babar and one of his triplets.

Materials: 40 x 22 cm of white Aida fabric with 14 thread groups per inch; 1.2 m x 90 cm white towelling; 5 m white bias binding; DMC embroidery threads listed.

Stitch count: 48H x 77W

Directions: Stitch the design in the centre of the Aida. Cut a 90 cm square of towelling and position the stitched design across one corner. Trim the short edges of the Aida to form a right-angled triangle. Cut an extra piece of towelling to match this. Round all corners and zigzag all edges.

KEY for Babar & baby			
	DMC	Colour	Stitches
■	310	black	34
+	350	rose	18
○	453	grey	556
×	702	green	1025
∪	793	blue	14
−	972	yellow	44
•		white	108
	310	black	backstitch

Sew the two triangles together with the design on top and bind the long edge with bias binding. Position this triangle on a corner of the towelling square, with the design face up, and sew along the two short edges. Finish the edges of the square with a length of bias binding.

Right: Height chart instructions are on p 40.

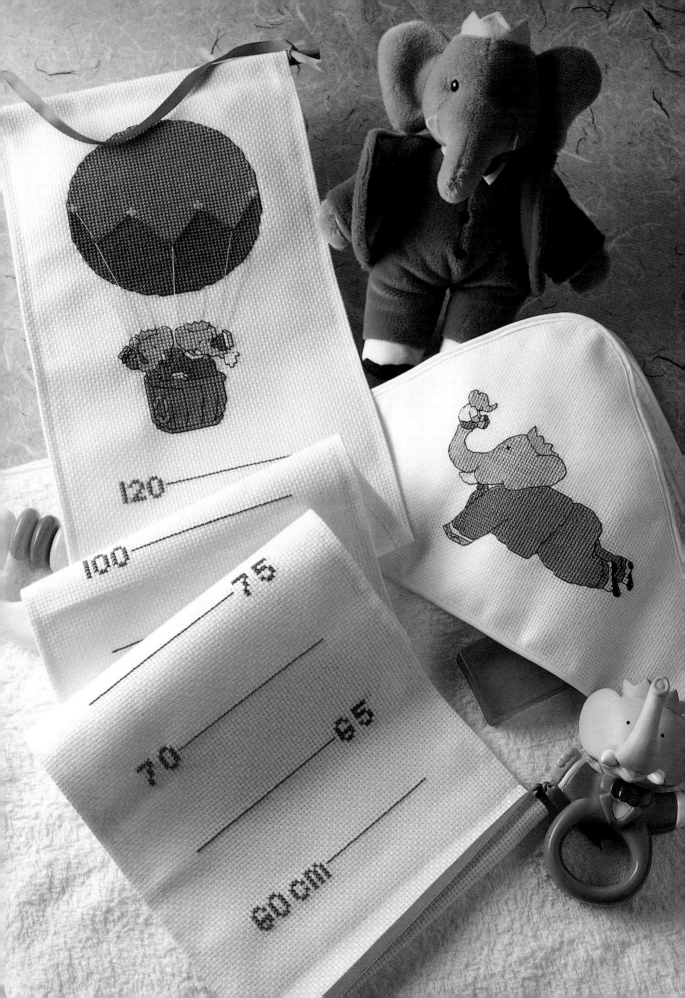

Height Chart

A height chart is an essential item in every child's room. Pin strips of ribbon as markers which can be moved up the chart over time.

Materials: 96 x 22 cm of white Aida fabric
with 11 thread groups per inch;
96 x 22 cm of white fabric;
green ribbon;
thin dowel;
metallic gold thread;
DMC embroidery threads listed.

Stitch count: 103H x 54W

Directions: Stitch the design at the top of the Aida fabric, allowing 7 cm above the balloon for the casing. Note that the dash lines are long stitches of gold thread. Cross-stitch '120 cm' 3 cm below the design at the left-hand side and backstitch a line across the chart (see pages 124-5). Cross-stitch '115 cm' 5 cm below, at the right-hand side, and add a backstitch line. Continue on down the chart, stitching each number 5 cm below the previous one, ending on '60 cm'. (The chart is hung above floor level.)

Zigzag the edges of the Aida fabric and carefully press the work. Back the Aida with the white fabric, turn over 1 cm along the long sides of the Aida, press, and sew 5 mm from the edge. Fold the top edge over 3 cm and sew across 2 cm from the fold to create a casing for the dowel. Repeat at the base.

Cut two 25 cm lengths of dowel and insert in the top and bottom casings. Cut a 40 cm piece of ribbon and tie each end to the ends of the top dowel, forming a hanging loop. Cut a piece of ribbon 30 cm in length and tie each end to the ends of the bottom dowel, securing it in place.

KEY for Babar's balloon			
	DMC	Colour	Stitches
*	350	rose	884
O	453	grey	191
+	702	green	1488
×	892	pink	81
−	972	yellow	74
∪	976	tan	280
•		white	38
Backstitch			
	310	black	solid lines
	972	gold	dash lines

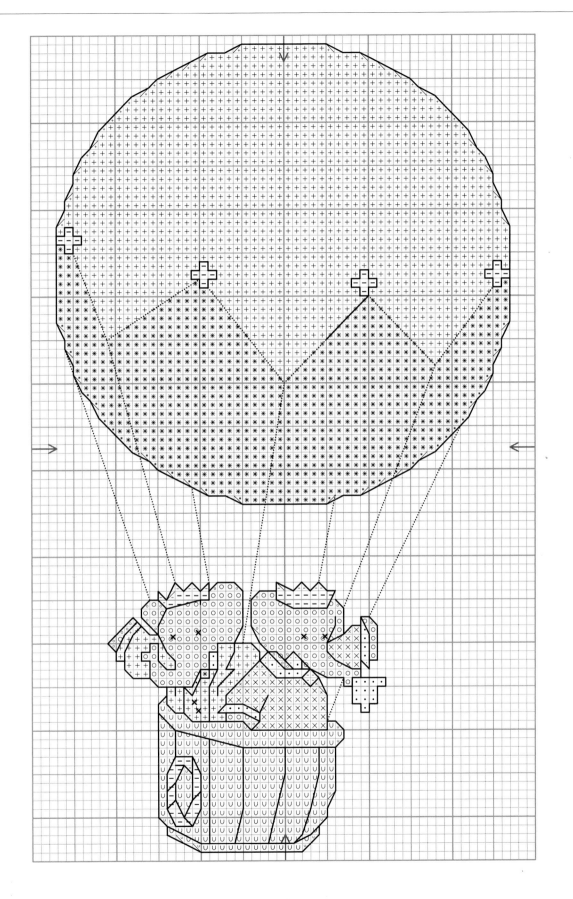

For Toddlers

*These early years
are a time of pure delight as
youngsters try their first steps,
learn their first words, and begin
to discover the joy of books. Here
are many characters who will
become firm friends: Spot, Miffy,
Paddington and the endearing
Duck, all used to decorate toys
and objects suitable for this age
group. Personalised gifts will become prized possessions with those
toddlers who have just learnt that
useful word "Mine!"*

Spot

The lovable puppy known as Spot first appeared on book-shelves in Eric Hill's award-winning Where's Spot? which was published in 1980. Within weeks the delightful lift-the-flap book was at the top of the bestseller list, leading to a whole series of stories about Spot. Eric Hill was a graphic designer and illustrator when he created the first Spot book to amuse his young son. The bright colours, gentle humour and intriguing design are a winning combination. Spot, whose favourite activities are hiding, exploring and opening presents, makes a wonderful introduction to the world of books. His adventures have been translated into over sixty languages, including Arabic, Manx and Urdu, and there are many dual-language editions such as English-Braille. All in all, over twenty million copies have been sold. Spot is also a multimedia star, appearing in his own animated series.

		KEY for Spot eating	
	DMC	Colour	Stitches
O	307	yellow	493
■	310	black	51
*	433	dark brown	71
+	725	gold	615
U	754	flesh	6
×	976	tan	65
	310	black	backstitch

Feeding Bib

Delight a special child with this image from Where's Spot?, one of the bestselling children's books ever to be published.

Materials: 25 x 30 cm of white Aida fabric with 14 thread groups per inch; 25 x 30 cm of white fabric; 2 m of red bias binding; DMC embroidery threads listed.

Stitch count: 35H x 58W

Directions: Stitch the design in the lower half of the Aida fabric. On a large piece of paper, draw the 23 x 28 cm bib shape, using the pattern on page 126 as a guide. Make sure the neck hole is large enough to fit the baby comfortably.

Pin the paper pattern onto the fabric and the backing, making sure that your design is in the correct position. Cut both fabrics in the bib shape. Remove the pattern and zigzag the fabric edges together.

Trim the outside edges with bias binding. Pin a 1 m strip of bias binding around the neckline so that the ties are of even length. Starting at one tie end, sew the bias binding edges together, continue sewing around the neckline and up to the end of the other tie.

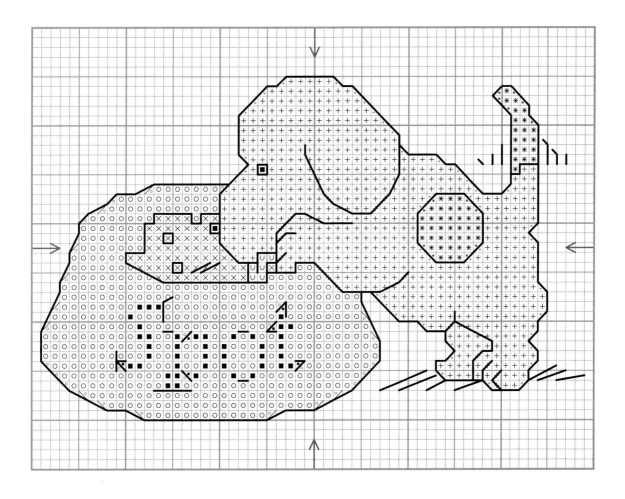

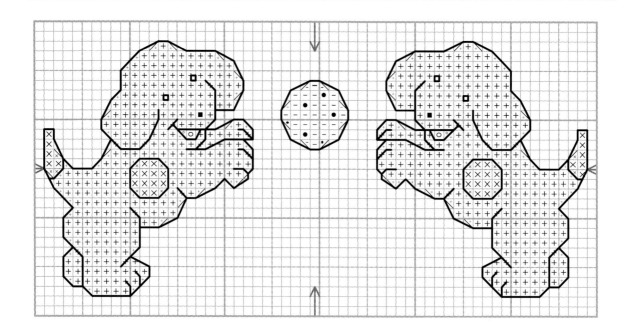

Towel Trim

This simple design of Spot at play is quick and easy to stitch. To adapt the motif for a longer trim, omit the mirrored figure and repeat the remaining design.

Materials: A handtowel;
a strip of white Aida fabric;
(or a towel with an Aida inset);
DMC embroidery threads listed.

Stitch count: 26H x 60W (adaptable)

Directions: Check the width of the towel and stitch the design so that the figures are evenly spaced. If making a band to apply to a towel, cut a strip of Aida fabric 2 cm wider than the width of the towel and stitch the design along the centre. Fold the raw edges to the back and press flat. Baste the strip onto your towel and then slipstitch along the edges, turning the ends in neatly. Press the towel carefully to complete.

	KEY for Spot and ball		
	DMC	Colour	Stitches
■	310	black	2
✕	433	dark brown	48
●	444	yellow	6
–	666	red	31
+	725	gold	610
○	754	flesh	4
	310	black	backstitch

Right: A handtowel and feeding bib make a delightful set. Instructions for the bib can be found on page 45.

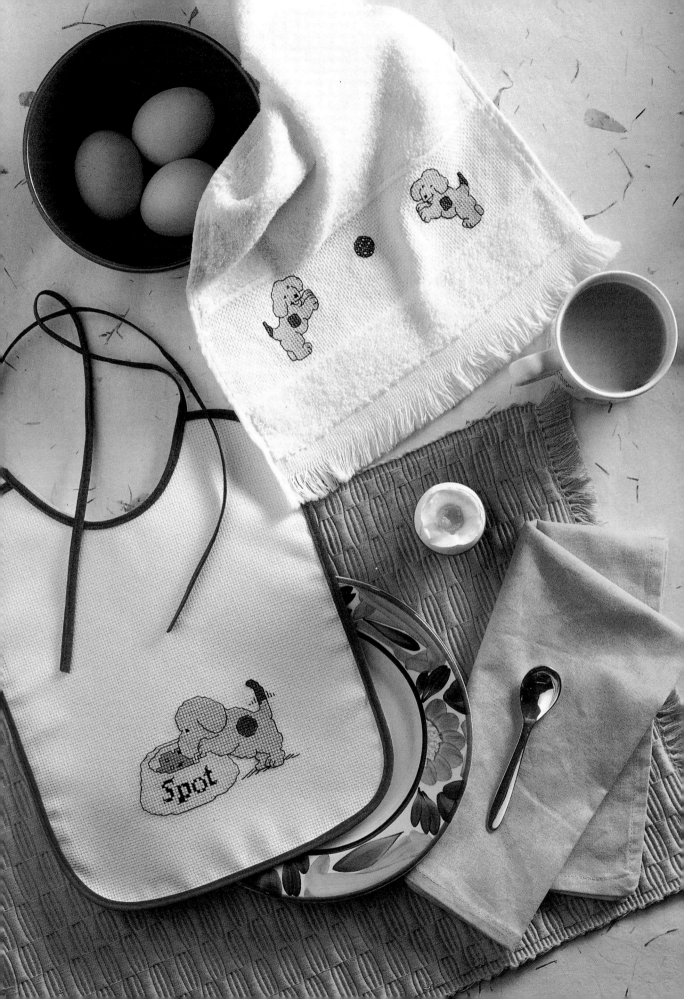

Artwork Folder

This colourful folder is ideal for securing a child's works of art. A photograph of the finished project can be found on page 51.

Materials: 20 x 25 cm of white Aida fabric
with 14 thread groups per inch;
34 x 51 cm heavy white card;
35 x 52 cm red card;
double-sided tape;
bookbinding tape;
DMC embroidery threads listed;
extra thread for cords.

Stitch count: 61H x 86W

	DMC	Colour	Stitches
■	310	black	11
‖	350	rose	90
X	433	dark brown	101
●	444	yellow	3
U	703	green	67
+	725	gold	1145
Z	754	flesh	6
O	798	blue	138
✱	918	rust	86
·	922	tan	879
▲	996	light blue	97
	310	black	backstitch

KEY for Spot painting

Directions: Stitch the design in the centre of the Aida fabric and press flat. Cut the white card into two pieces, each 34 x 25.5 cm. Lay one on top of the other and use bookbinding tape to tape them together along one long edge. Position double-sided tape on one side of the folder and stick down the stitched design so that it is centred.

Cut three lengths of embroidery thread, each 50 cm, plait them and tie a knot 1 cm up from each end. Cut the plait in half and knot the ends; you should have two cords. Tape one cord in the centre of the top edge of both the front and the back card.

Cut the red card into two pieces, each one 26 x 35 cm in size. Cut a window, 18 x 14 cm in one piece of card to frame the cross-stitch. Stick double-sided tape at the edges of the white card and around the window on the red card. Position the red card over the design and stick it down. Cover the back with the second sheet of red card. Trim the edges of the red card to fit the white cards. Tie the cords to complete.

Diagram of Artwork Folder showing the boards, binding tape, cords, cross-stitch and covering card.

Right: An attractive folder is ideal for safekeeping the best pictures created by a child. The chart and instructions for making this can be found on pages 48-9.

Below: This sturdy bag will hold plenty of special picture books. Instructions begin on page 52.

Book Bag

Every child needs a bag in which to carry their Spot books. This one will also fit larger picture books and is ideal for trips to the library. It is pictured on page 50.

Materials: 25 x 30 cm of white Aida fabric with 14 thread groups per inch; 25 x 30 cm of white fabric; 1 m x 50 cm coloured fabric; coloured bias binding; DMC embroidery threads listed.

Stitch count: 70H x 67W

Directions: Stitch the design on the Aida fabric so that the 30 cm edges form the top and bottom. Carefully press the finished stitching.

Cut the Aida into a flap, 27 cm wide and 22 cm high, with the design 3 cm from the bottom edge. Round off the bottom two corners and cut a matching piece of white fabric as backing. Zigzag the edges of both layers to prevent fraying and sew coloured bias binding around the sides and base.

Cut a piece of coloured fabric measuring 68 cm x 30 cm to make the body of the bag. Zigzag all edges. Sew a 4 cm hem along one short edge. Align the other short edge with the untrimmed edge of the flap section and sew the Aida and coloured fabric together with right sides facing. Press the seam and handsew the edge of the white backing fabric down to cover it.

Cut two strips of coloured fabric, each 32 x 5 cm, to form the sides of the bag. Zigzag all edges and sew a 1 cm hem at one short edge of each strip. Lay a strip along one edge of the body section so that the hemmed end is aligned with the start of the Aida flap. Sew the side strip onto the body section, with right sides facing. Repeat at the other side.

To make the handle, cut a strip of coloured fabric, 75 x 7 cm and zigzag the raw edges. Fold the piece in half lengthwise and sew a 1 cm seam to form a long fabric tube. Turn the tube inside out and press flat. Handsew each end inside the bag sides, allowing a 2.5 cm overlap for strength.

	DMC	Colour	Stitches
	*	310	black	5
•	350	rose	351
✕	433	brown	95
∪	444	yellow	47
○	721	orange	431
+	725	gold	1312
<	905	green	120
▲	3765	blue	41
	310	black	backstitch

KEY for Spot reading

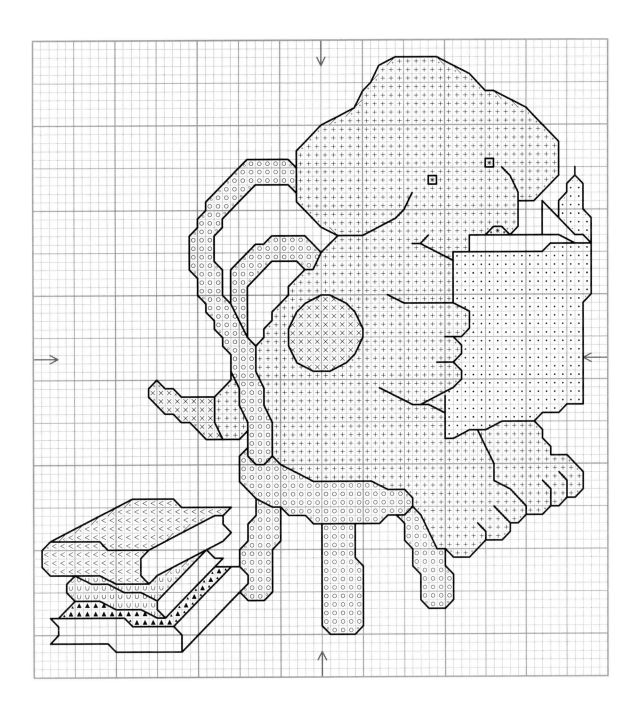

Miffy

Kitty

Miffy

The simple lines and bright colours that distinguish Miffy and her friends from other characters are the trademark of Dick Bruna, a remarkably innovative artist and author. Bruna was born in Utrecht in the Netherlands in 1927 and even as a small child he enjoyed drawing. His first book was published in 1953 and it introduced a new concept in books for the young, designed as it was for the child, rather than the parent. Bruna created Miffy, one of his most popular characters, after watching his own children play with a pet rabbit. His use of bold, contrasting colours has since been adopted by other illustrators, but none has achieved the same worldwide success. Dick Bruna's books, which include a whole series of Miffy adventures, have been translated into many languages from the original Dutch and have recently been animated for television. Miffy, Pussy Nell and Snuffy are today as enchanting to his young audience as they were forty years ago.

Napkin Ring

Pussy Nell features here on a napkin ring. She could also be used on other party items, such as crackers, name tags and placemats.

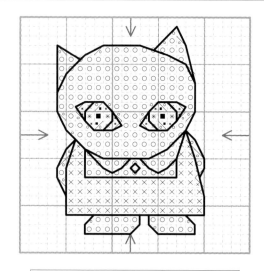

Materials: 20 x 10 cm of white Aida fabric
with 14 thread groups per inch;
5 cm wide white Aida band;
a cardboard or plastic tube;
double-sided tape;
DMC embroidery threads listed.

Stitch count: 22H x 16W

Directions: Stitch the design in the centre of the Aida fabric, with short edges at the top and bottom. Zigzag the edges to prevent fraying. Find a cardboard tube large enough to hold a napkin and cut a section 5 cm wide. Wind double-sided tape around the outside of the tube and cover it with the Aida fabric. Handsew the overlapping end. Fold the edges inside the tube and handsew the two edges with a lacing stitch. Cut a piece of Aida band to fit inside the tube and handsew it in place.

KEY for Miffy and Pussy Nell			
	DMC	Colour	Stitches
■	310	black	6
+	444	yellow	94
＊	701	green	20
×	797	blue	98
○		white	410
	310	black	backstitch

Gift Sack

There are a thousand uses for this bright little sack, which takes only a few minutes to make up once Miffy has been stitched.

Materials: 32 x 12 cm of red Aida fabric
with 14 thread groups per inch;
ribbon;
DMC embroidery threads listed.

Stitch count: 26H x 25W

Directions: Fold the fabric in half to form a 16 x 12 cm rectangle. Stitch the design 2.5 cm from the folded base. With the design facing inwards, sew the side seams and zigzag all edges to prevent fraying. Turn the bag inside out. Fold over and sew a 1 cm hem at the opening. Fill the sack with small treats and tie it closed with a ribbon.

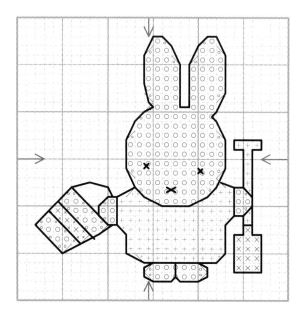

Pyjamas

Cross-stitching over waste canvas is a great way to decorate plain clothes. Here a cherub from the original Miffy book adorns an inexpensive top.

Materials: 18 x 18 cm of waste canvas
with 6.5 thread groups per inch;
blue fleecy top and pants;
DMC embroidery threads listed.

Stitch count: 52H x 53W

Directions: Position the waste canvas on the front of the top, ensuring that it is squared up. Tack around the edges and diagonally so that the canvas is securely attached. Stitch the design, using three strands of embroidery thread. When stitching is complete, remove tacking thread, dampen canvas with a cloth and carefully pull out the waste canvas strands.

Alternatively, this design could be stitched on blue Aida fabric.

	KEY for cherub		
	DMC	Colour	Stitches
×	972	yellow	197
○		white	870
	310	black	backstitch

Above: All children are angels when they're asleep. The pattern for this quick project appears on page 57.

Illustrations Dick Bruna, © copyright Mercis b.v., 1963

Right: A set of finger puppets on a stand will give small children hours of simple fun. Instructions are on page 61.

Illustrations Dick Bruna,
© copyright Mercis b.v., 1974

Finger Puppets

Dick Bruna has a wonderful way of simplifying the adult world. This collection of sailor, farmer, knight, clown and town mayor make ideal finger puppets for small people, as pictured on page 59.

Materials: 12 x 12 cm of Aida fabric with 14 thread groups per inch; white backing fabric; coloured cotton fabric; DMC embroidery threads listed.

Stitch count: approximately 45H x 25W

Directions: Stitch each design on a piece of Aida fabric. For each puppet, cut two 12 cm squares of backing fabric and one of coloured cotton. Lay the cross-stitching face down on a backing square and sew along the base, 5 mm below the bottom row of cross-stitches. Trim the edge and zigzag it, then turn the piece inside out so that the design faces out and is backed with the white fabric. Baste 5 mm around the figure, stitching the layers together.

Sew the other backing square and the coloured square together along one side, forming the base. Trim the edge and zigzag, then turn the piece inside out.

Place the two sections together with the bases aligned and with the cross-stitching and coloured fabric facing each other. Sew them together, using the basted outline as a guide. Trim the edges and zigzag to secure threads. Turn the puppet inside out and use a teaspoon to shape the head.

To make a puppet stand, drill holes in a narrow block of timber and glue in short sections of dowel.

KEY for Bruna people			
	DMC	*Colour*	*Stitches*
■	310	black	653
O	318	grey	581
−	702	green	500
X	798	blue	613
+	946	orange	1020
U	973	yellow	615
<	976	brown	66
•		white	137
	310	black	backstitch

Paddington

There have been many bears in children's stories but the figure of a small furry bear in a duffle coat and battered hat can only conjure up one name: Paddington. This charming bear with a great fondness for marmalade was found one day on London's Paddington Station by the kind-hearted Mr and Mrs Brown. Paddington's Aunt Lucy in Peru had taken the precaution of tying a luggage label around his neck which read "please look after this bear" and so he joined the Brown household at number thirty-two Windsor Gardens. When Michael Bond wrote A Bear Called Paddington in the late 1950s, he created a wonderful character who could turn ordinary activities— having a bath, home decorating, visiting the cinema—into quite extraordinary happenings. Further adventures kept children vastly amused and a series of picture books based on the character made Paddington a firm favourite with even the very young. Any bear who keeps a trusty marmalade sandwich under his hat in case of emergencies has to be a little bit special.

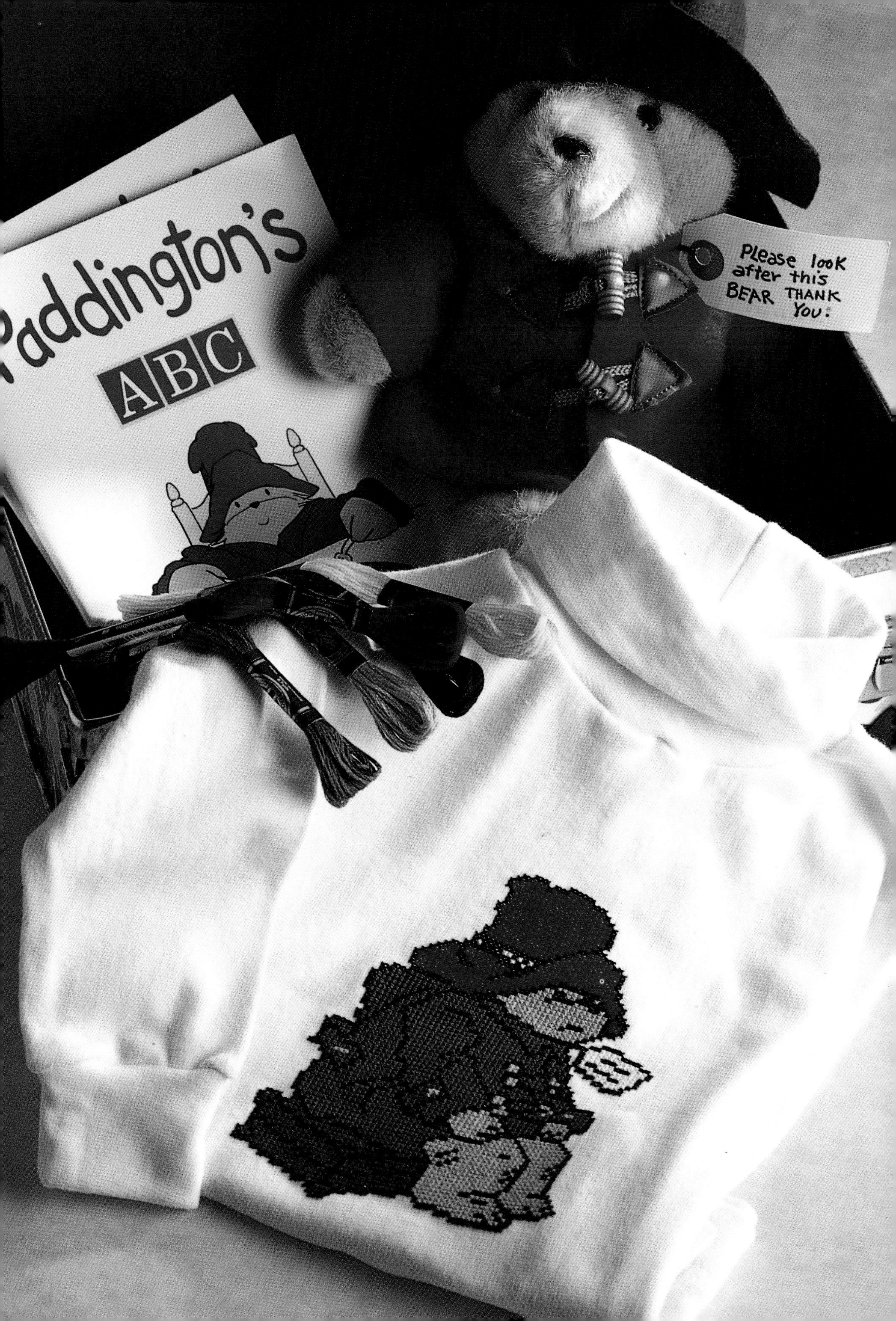
Paddington's
ABC
Please look after this BEAR THANK YOU!

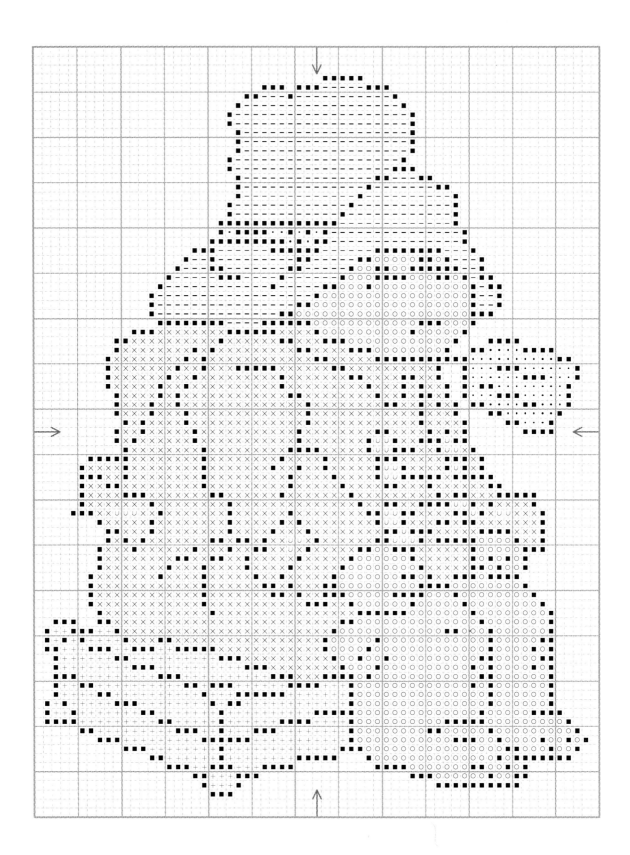

Child's Top

The quintessential image of Paddington is this one: newly arrived from darkest Peru and sitting on his suitcase. In place of back-stitching, this design has an outline of black cross-stitches. Page 63 pictures it stitched onto a ready-made top.

Materials: 25 x 30 cm of waste canvas
with 14 thread groups per inch;
a white t-shirt or top;
DMC embroidery threads listed.

Stitch count: 80H x 63W

Directions: Position the waste canvas on the front of the top, ensuring that it is squared up. Tack around the edges and diagonally so that the canvas is securely attached.

Stitch the design, using two strands of embroidery thread. When stitching is complete, remove the tacking threads, dampen the canvas with a cloth and slowly pull out the strands of the waste canvas. Carefully press the finished garment.

	DMC	Colour	Stitches
■	310	black	1454
+	300	russet	737
○	422	light brown	1527
−	666	red	1171
×	797	blue	2574
∪	972	gold	71
·		white	159

KEY for Paddington seated

Placemat

Paddington's dreams of marmalade will brighten any breakfast table.

Materials: 21 x 21 cm of cream Aida fabric with 11 thread groups per inch; DMC embroidery threads listed.

Stitch count: 53H x 53W

Directions: Stitch the design on the Aida fabric. Zigzag around the placemat, 1 cm in from each edge, using cream thread. Pull the threads of the Aida to form a 1 cm fringe. For extra durability, have the mat laminated.

	DMC	Colour	Stitches
■	310	black	14
✳	321	dark red	39
O	422	light brown	289
U	436	brown	31
+	444	yellow	287
X	666	red	952
–	740	orange	52
•	745	cream	30
	310	black	backstitch

KEY for Paddington dreaming

KEY for Paddington shopping

	DMC	Colour	Stitches
■	310	black	17
✳	321	dark red	69
○	422	light brown	277
Z	435	brown	64
·	648	grey	52
N	666	red	222
✕	702	green	7
−	740	orange	75
<	745	cream	68
+	797	blue	588
∪	972	gold	8
	310	black	backstitch

Shopping Bag

This handy bag, which features Paddington stocking up on his favourite delicacy, appears on page 68. For extra strength, line the bag with a waterproof material.

Materials: 62 x 28 cm of cream Aida fabric with 11 thread groups per inch; 70 cm of 2.5 cm wide cream tape; DMC embroidery threads listed.

Stitch count: 54H x 54W

Directions: Zigzag the edges of the Aida fabric to prevent fraying. Sew a 2 cm hem at both of the narrow ends. Stitch the design so that the top of the figure starts 7 cm below one of the hemmed edges. Press the stitched fabric carefully.

On each hemmed edge of the cloth, mark two points, each 8.5 cm in from the sides. To form the handles, cut two pieces of the cream tape, each 35 cm long, and sew a 2 cm hem at each end. Pin each end of one length of tape onto one of the hemmed edges at the two marked points. Sew around the overlap and diagonally so that the tape is attached securely to the bag. Repeat on the other hemmed edge.

Fold the fabric in half with the design face up and the two hemmed edges aligned. Pin the two layers of fabric at each side, at a point 5 cm up from the folded edge. Turn the front flap over and the bottom flap under so that the design is now inside the bag and there is a valley fold in the base. Sew a 1 cm seam along the two sides. Turn the completed bag inside out.

Diagram of Shopping Bag showing the folded Aida fabric with pins 5 cm up from the folded edge.

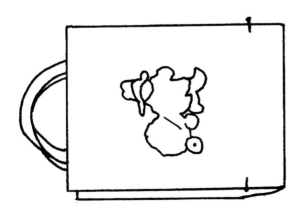

The bag with the front folded over and the back folded under to make a valley fold in the base.

A small shopping bag is ideal for
a small person. The instructions
and chart for this design can be
found on the previous pages.

An apron is useful for cooking, craft-
work, gardening or any number of
things. Instructions start on page 72.

KEY for Paddington gardening

	DMC	Colour	Stitches
■	310	black	14
+	422	brown	298
✕	666	red	596
N	703	green	54
✱	720	burnt orange	12
U	741	orange	155
○	797	blue	231
−	972	gold	27
	310	black	backstitch

Child's Apron

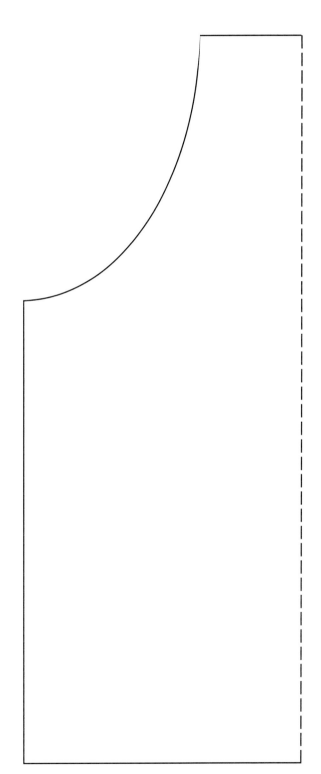

Paddington is one of those bears who likes to be helpful but who inevitably creates havoc. For some tasks an apron, like the one shown on page 71, is indispensible.

Materials: 18 x 18 cm of cream Aida fabric
with 11 thread groups per inch;
18 x 18 cm cream backing fabric;
55 x 55 cm coloured fabric;
3 m of contrasting bias binding;
DMC embroidery threads listed.

Stitch count: 54H x 57W

Directions: Stitch the design on the Aida fabric and press the finished work. Back this with a square of light-coloured fabric and trim the edges with bias binding: this section will be the apron pocket.

On a large piece of paper, draw up the apron shape using the pattern on the right as a guide. The height should be 55 cm and the half-width 22 cm.

Fold the square of coloured fabric in half and pin the paper pattern onto the fabric, so that the dashed line is on the folded edge. Cut the fabric in the apron shape. Remove the pattern and zigzag the fabric edges to prevent fraying.

Sew a 1 cm hem on each straight edge. Pin a 210 cm piece of bias binding along the armhole curves to form a neck loop and apron ties. Make sure the ties are of even length. Starting at one tie end, sew the bias binding edges together, sew the bias binding around the armhole curves and continue sewing to the other end of the tie.

Position the pocket on the front of the apron, 4 cm from the top hem. With a cream thread, sew along the sides and base of the Aida fabric, securing the pocket in place.

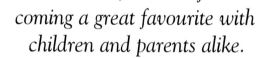 Duck

Stephen Cartwright's Duck is featured in over thirty Usborne books, including the bestselling First Thousand Words in which he made his first appearance. Often he is discreetly hidden on the page for the eager child to discover, but occasionally he stars in his very own book, along with his friends. He is really more duckling than duck and small children delight in his playful and sometimes mischievous ways. A slight inclination of the beak, a minor adjustment of the dotty eyes, and Duck bears a totally new expression. Duck's exploits are simple ones—going to the seaside, meeting up with new friends—but Cartwright's attention to detail makes every picture a story in itself. Indeed, the books are designed to encourage children to name objects and talk about actions while enjoying themselves. A relative newcomer to the world of children's books, Duck is fast becoming a great favourite with children and parents alike.

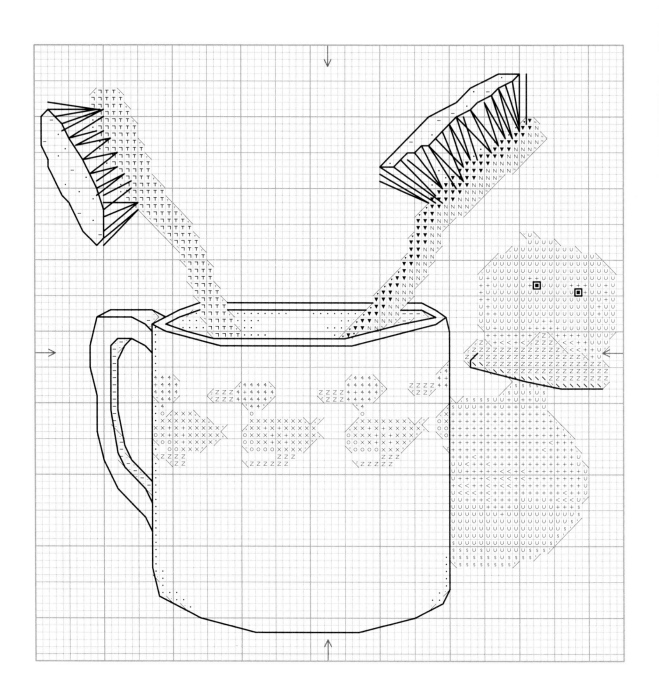

Wash Bag

Pictured on page 75 is a useful bag to take to nursery school or when visiting overnight at grandma's house. To make it extra handy, you could line it with a waterproof material.

Materials: 20 x 20 cm of white Aida fabric with 14 thread groups per inch; 20 x 20 cm white backing fabric; 60 x 30 cm coloured fabric; 70 cm strong cord; DMC embroidery threads listed.

Stitch count: 78H x 84W

Directions: Stitch the design in the centre of the Aida fabric and carefully press. Back with a piece of white fabric the same size. Cut four strips of coloured fabric: a top panel and bottom panel each measuring 8 x 18 cm, and two side panels each 5 x 27 cm. Cut a 27 x 24 cm piece for the back of the bag. Zigzag the edges of all pieces to prevent fraying.

Lay the top and bottom strips on the Aida with right sides facing and sew a 1 cm seam. Press seams flat and repeat with the side panels. Place the front and back sections together, right sides facing, and sew a 1 cm seam along the sides and base. Turn the neck of the bag over twice to create a casing deep enough for the cord. Sew the bottom of the casing, stopping 1 cm short of your starting point.

Attach a safety pin to one end of the cord and push it through the 1 cm gap and into the casing. Thread the cord right around the casing and push it back out through the gap. Remove the pin. Tie the cord ends tightly.

KEY for Duck & toothbrushes			
	DMC	Colour	Stitches
<	307	lemon	40
■	310	black	2
–	414	dark grey	59
·	415	light grey	127
+	444	yellow	281
×	517	teal	124
\	606	flame	21
Z	608	orange	138
⌐	666	red	95
4	701	dark green	66
O	704	light green	30
S	782	tan	58
▼	797	dark blue	93
N	798	blue	99
T	817	dark red	96
U	972	gold	345
Backstitch			
	817	dark red	mouth
	310	black	other details

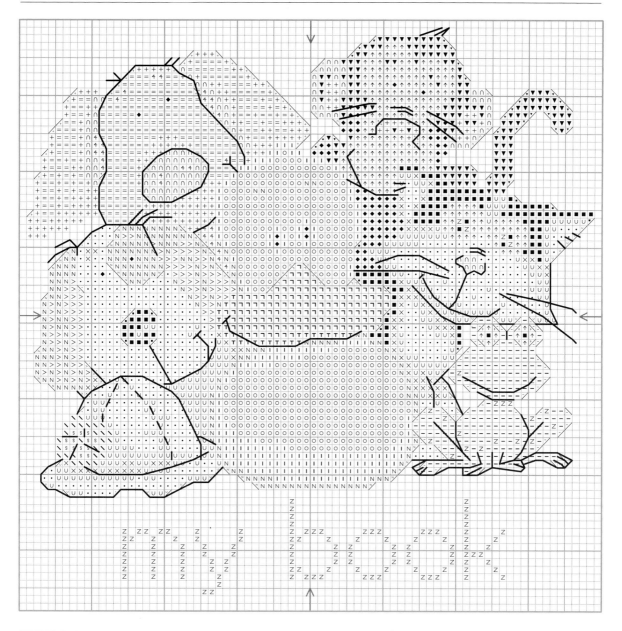

KEY for Cover	78H x 78W			DMC	Colour	Stitches		DMC	Colour	Stitches
	DMC	Colour	Stitches	s	604	pink	13	I	972	gold	195
▼	300	brown	188	˥	606	orange	150	•		white	525
■	310	black	132	T	666	red	27				
∩	353	apricot	125	Z	701	green	138	*Backstitch*			
>	400	red brown	98	↑	745	pale yellow	235	300	brown	monkey, duck
4	407	mushroom	39	+	754	flesh	250	400	red brown	dog hairs
✕	414	grey	88	N	782	tan	228	407	mushroom	pig
U	415	light grey	280	−	907	lime green	251	601	crimson	flower
o	444	yellow	525	◆	938	dark brown	84	701	green	frog
\	601	crimson	28	=	951	cream	294	414	grey	other details

Cloth Book

This enchanting book opens to show each animal and its name. The designs are so sweet that you might reuse them in other projects.

Materials: 1 m x 60 cm of white Aida fabric with 14 thread groups per inch; thin white backing fabric; thin wadding; green ribbon and sewing thread; DMC embroidery threads listed.

Directions: To make the full book, cut fourteen pieces of Aida fabric, each 20 cm square. On one square, stitch the cover design which is shown on page 78. Then stitch each animal on a different square.

Stitch the name of each animal on an Aida square, using the chart on page 126.

Cut fourteen matching pieces of fine white backing fabric and back each Aida square with a piece. Cut seven matching pieces of thin wadding. Construct each 'page' with an animal on one side and a word on the other and a piece of wadding in between. Make sure the sequence is correct so that facing pages match the name to the appropriate animal. Tack around the edges to secure the layers in place.

Zigzag the top, right-hand edge and bottom with 4 mm stitches in green thread. Repeat to create an edging of solid colour. Bind the book by folding the left-hand edges of the cover and back page in between the centre pages. Sew along the spine with a heavy-duty needle. Decorate with a ribbon.

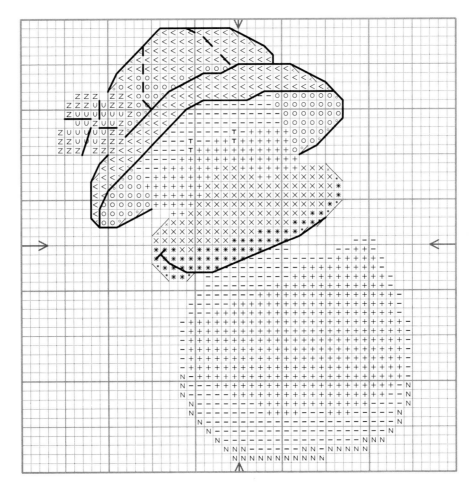

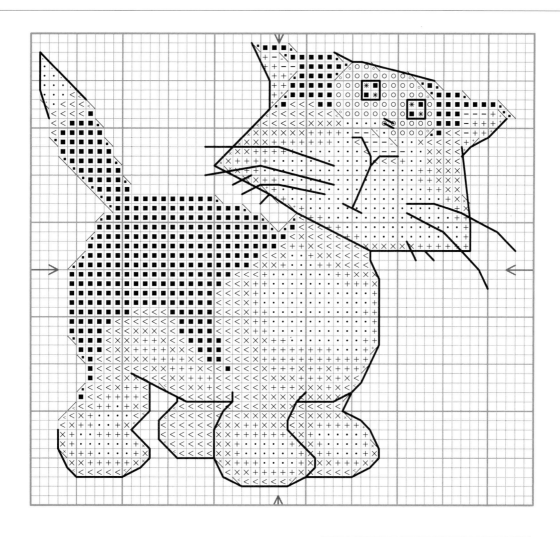

KEY for duck		48H x 41W
DMC	Colour	Stitches
O 415	grey	93
+ 444	yellow	410
Z 601	crimson	29
U 604	pink	20
× 606	orange	115
✳ 666	red	59
N 782	tan	38
T 938	brown	4
– 972	gold	250
<	white	168
Backstitch		
414	grey	hat
601	crimson	flower
938	brown	beak

KEY for cat		47H x 52W
DMC	Colour	Stitches
■ 310	black	390
– 353	apricot	21
< 413	dark grey	256
× 414	grey	175
+ 415	light grey	230
✳ 701	green	4
O 745	cream	59
•	white	301
310	black	backstitch

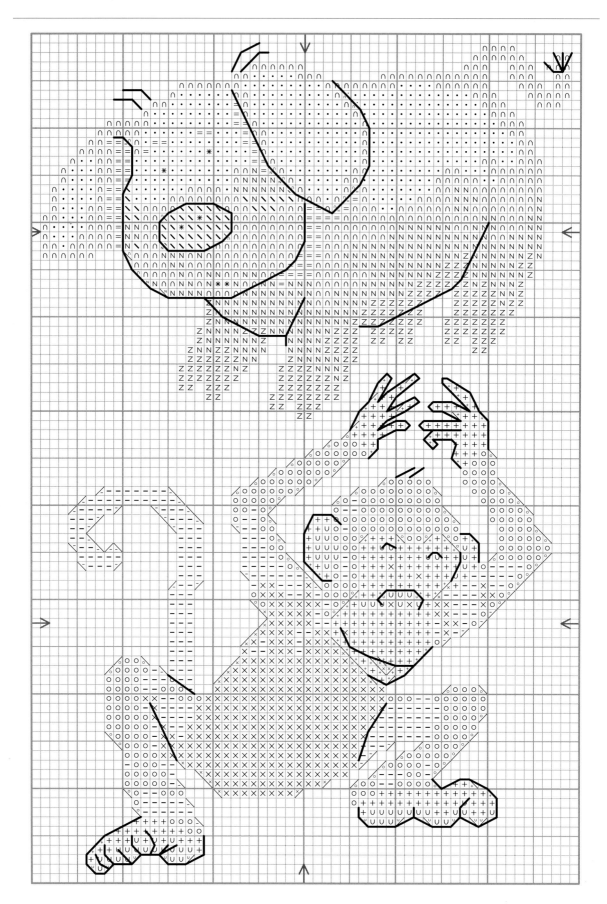

KEY for pig		40H x 58W
DMC	Colour	Stitches
\ 353	pink	48
= 407	mushroom	65
Z 452	light grey	182
N 453	dark grey	274
∩ 754	apricot	451
* 839	brown	6
• 951	cream	401
839	brown	backstitch

KEY for monkey		53H x 53W
DMC	Colour	Stitches
− 300	light brown	290
O 400	red brown	386
+ 745	cream	260
X 898	brown	352
U 950	apricot	74
898	brown	backstitch

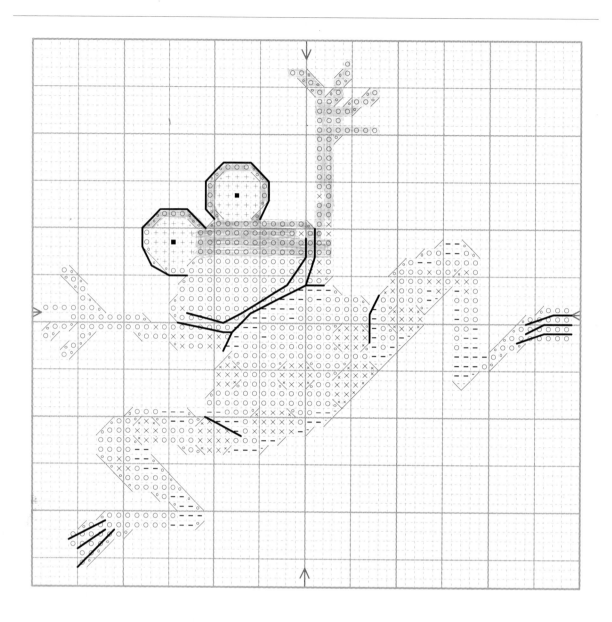

KEY for frog		54H x 58W	
	DMC	Colour	Stitches
■	310	black	2
×	701	emerald	132
−	703	green	112
+	745	cream	48
○	907	lime green	629
	701	emerald	backstitch

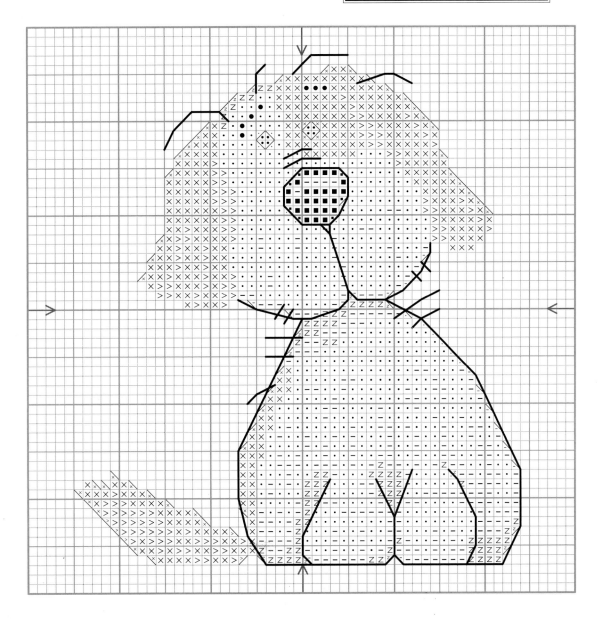

KEY for dog   53H x 49W

	DMC	Colour	Stitches
■	310	black	33
Z	318	dark grey	91
>	400	brown	116
–	415	light grey	265
×	782	tan	367
●	938	dark brown	15
·		white	639

Backstitch
	400	brown	head hairs
	310	black	other detail

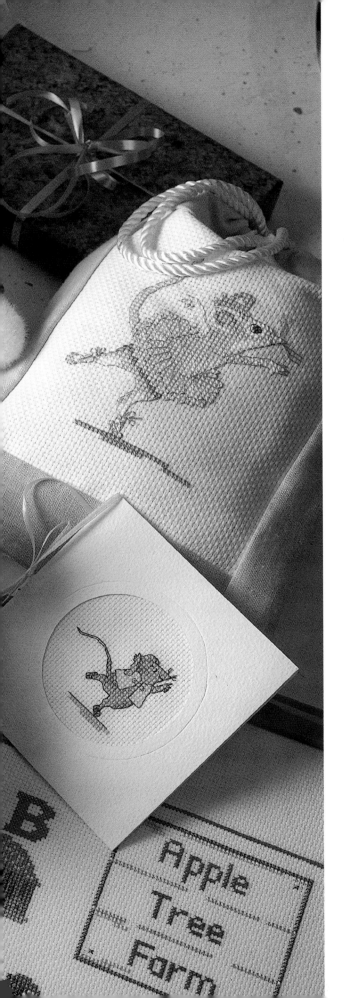

Growing Up

The school years bring a range of exciting things to learn and do. Here are lots of gifts to make those years even more enjoyable: small people will love practising the alphabet with Apple Tree Farm, attending dance classes with Angelina, and adventuring with Rupert and the ever-youthful Peter Pan. Cross-stitch can be used to decorate an infinite number of things—pencil cases, sports bags, T-shirts, beach towels—all of which will appeal to older children.

Peter Pan

Sir James Barrie was born in Scotland in 1860. His boyish imagination thrived on tales of desert islands, pirates, and Indian warriors as, with his friends, he played out many adventures. These images reappeared much later in many of his plays and stories. Barrie's own marriage was childless but he formed close friendships with other people's children, in particular with the Llewelyn Davies family of five boys. In 1902 he wrote a story for the oldest boy entitled The Little White Bird in which the character of Peter Pan first appeared. Later, when Barrie and his wife, Mary Ansell, bought a home in Surrey, the boys came to stay and played out the stories which Barrie so loved to tell them. From these shared adventures grew the world-famous play Peter Pan which was first produced in London in December 1904. It made household names of such characters as Wendy, Tinker Bell and the wicked Captain Hook. Peter Pan, the hero, is at times a little selfish and at others delightfully naive.

The boy who never grew up nonetheless grew in popularity and continues to live on in the hearts of children—of all ages.

KEY for Peter Pan

	DMC	Colour	Stitches
■	310	black	21
✳	610	brown	81
○	701	dark green	296
✕	703	green	323
−	907	lime	149
·	928	smoke	368
∪	945	tan	219
+	948	flesh	389
<	3072	light smoke	347
▲	3712	pink	2

Backstitch

928	smoke	shadow
3371	chocolate	other details

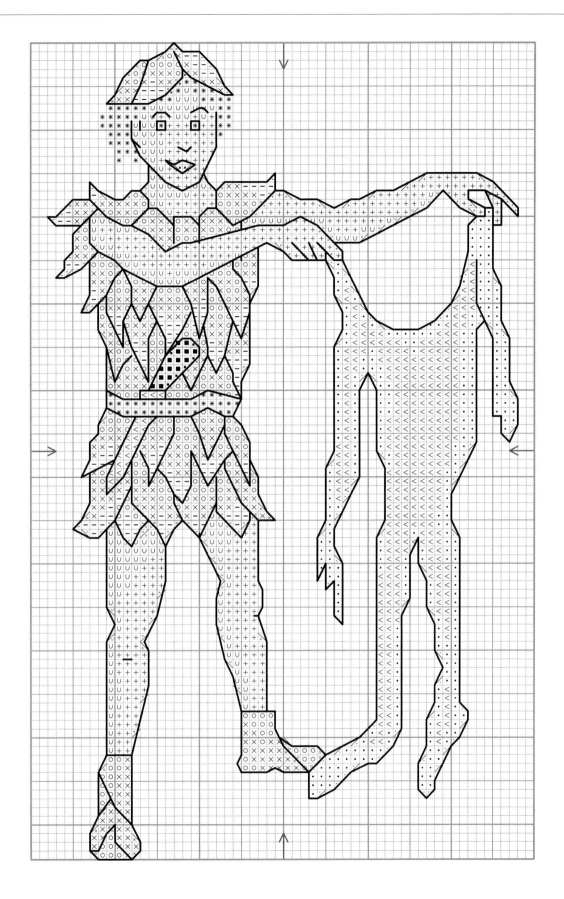

Pyjama Case ☆ ★ ☆

This design, pictured above, shows Peter with his shadow (before Wendy sews it back on).

Materials: 35 x 35 cm cream linen
with 30 threads per inch;
2 squares (35 cm) backing fabric;
35 x 35 cm coloured fabric;
Velcro® strips; ribbon;
DMC embroidery threads listed.

Stitch count: 94H x 56W

Directions: Stitch the design in the centre of the linen. Zigzag all fabric pieces. Lay the stitched design face down on a backing square and sew a 1 cm seam along one edge. Turn inside out and press the seam. Sew the coloured fabric and other backing square in the same way. Lay the two sections together with right sides facing and seamed edges aligned. Sew a 1 cm seam around the other three edges. Handsew strips of Velcro® onto either side of the opening. Turn the case inside out and press.

Album ☆ ☆ ☆ ☆ ☆ ☆ ☆ ☆ ☆ ☆

Tinker Bell, possibly the best-known fairy in the world, adorns this album cover. The pages, cut from coloured card, could hold a collection of special photographs or cards.

Materials: 35 x 60 cm of white linen
with 30 threads per inch;
sturdy white card;
thin coloured card;
thin wadding;
1.5 m of 3 mm wide ribbon;
DMC embroidery threads listed.

Stitch count: 86H x 76W

Directions: Cut the linen into two pieces, each 35 x 30 cm and zigzag the edges. With the long edges as the top and bottom, stitch the design in the centre of one of the linen rectangles. Carefully press the finished work.

Cut two pieces of card, each 27 x 22 cm. Mark a line 3.5 cm in from the short edge on one piece and score it with a knife. Cut a piece of thin wadding 23.5 x 22 cm and glue it onto the card, to the right of the scored line. Position the stitched work over the wadding, fold the edges over and secure them with pins at the back. Lace the top and bottom with strong thread and then lace the two sides. Glue a piece of coloured card over the lacing. With a knife, make two cuts along the spine, each 5 mm, in the same position as the holes created by a two-hole punch. Apply glue around the cuts to prevent the linen from fraying.

Make the back cover in the same way, but using the unstitched piece of linen. Cut pages of coloured card 5 mm smaller than the covers and punch holes along one side.

KEY for Tinker Bell			
	DMC	Colour	Stitches
X	340	mauve	242
N	341	blue	533
+	369	green	179
✳	402	bronze	79
Z	743	gold	14
−	945	flesh	115
<	948	apricot	109
U	3713	pink	210
O	3747	pale blue	540

Backstitch		
301	brown	hair
340	mauve	dress & pupils
743	gold	stars & wandshine
3328	red	mouth
317	grey	other details

Cut a 50 cm length of ribbon and thread it through the slots in the back cover, the holes in the pages, and up through the front cover slots. Tie the ribbon in a tight bow to bind the album securely.

Cut pieces of ribbon to form a frame on the front cover, cutting the ends at an angle to form mitred corners. Glue them in place on the linen. If the album will be handled often, you may wish to spray the covers with a protective coating.

Angelina

Angelina danced her way into children's hearts a decade or so ago and has been making repeat curtain calls ever since. Her debut was suitably entitled Angelina Ballerina and was written by Katharine Holabird and illustrated by Helen Craig. It tells the tale of a young mouse who dreams of being a ballerina and, after causing a fair amount of havoc around the house, is given a present of ballet lessons by her parents, Mr and Mrs Mouseling. Angelina proved such a success that she twirled into many further adventures which introduced other family members such as the delightful Cousin Henry. Helen Craig's fine illustrations are perfectly executed, endowing a white mouse with all the characteristics of a good-natured and excitable little girl. In a very short space of time, Holabird and Craig's widely acclaimed books have become contemporary classics for young readers.

Ballet Bag

This elegant drawstring bag can be used to hold ballet shoes, favourite slippers or any personal treasures. The example on page 95 is made of multiple panels, but you could also appliqué the stitched design onto a finished bag.

Materials: 19 x 19 cm of white Aida fabric with 14 thread groups per inch; 19 x 19 cm white backing fabric; 60 x 35 cm of coloured fabric; satin cord; DMC embroidery threads listed.

Stitch count: 55H x 48W

Directions: Stitch the design in the centre of the Aida fabric. Back with a piece of white fabric cut to the same size then trim 1 cm off all the sides. Zigzag the edges.

Cut four strips of coloured fabric: a top panel measuring 17.5 x 9 cm, a bottom panel of 17.5 x 7 cm, and two side panels each 6 x 32 cm. Cut a piece for the back of the bag, 24.5 x 32 cm. Zigzag the edges of all pieces to prevent fraying.

Lay the top and bottom strips on the Aida with right sides facing and sew a 1 cm seam. Press seams flat and repeat with the side panels. Place the front and back sections together, right sides facing, and sew a 1 cm seam along the sides and base. Turn the neck of the bag over twice to create a casing deep enough for the cord. Sew the bottom edge of the casing, stopping 1 cm short of your starting point.

Knot one end of the cord. Attach a safety pin to the other end of the cord and push it through the 1 cm gap and into the casing. Thread the cord right around the casing and push it back out through the gap. Remove the pin and tie a knot in the end of the cord.

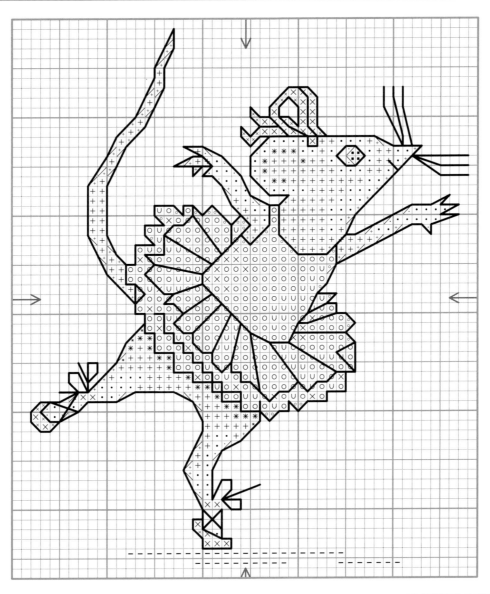

		KEY for Angelina	
	DMC	Colour	Stitches
■	317	dark grey	4
✳	318	grey	28
–	471	green	40
✕	761	peach	72
+	762	light grey	197
U	819	pale pink	61
O	963	pink	281
•		white	118

Backstitch

317	dark grey	eye & mouth
318	grey	other details

Door Plate (page 100) and
Congratulations Card (page 101)

Angelina Baller

Door Plate

Angelina pirouettes her way into a slight faux pas in this charming design, shown on page 99. If you wish to add a child's name, allow for extra fabric and card.

Materials: 50 x 25 cm of white linen
with 27 threads per inch;
38 x 15 cm of white card;
narrow pink ribbon;
strong cotton thread;
DMC embroidery threads listed.

Stitch count: 33H x 173W

Directions: Zigzag the edges of the linen to prevent fraying. Stitch the design in the centre of the linen adding a name if desired. Carefully press the finished work.

Cut a sturdy piece of card and lay the stitched design over it, making sure it is straight. Fold the edges of the fabric over and secure it with pins at the back. Starting at the top left, lace the top and bottom edges with strong thread. Repeat this with the two side edges.

Cut four pieces of ribbon: two 35 cm lengths and two 12 cm lengths. Cut the ends at an angle and glue the pieces onto the front of the panel to frame the design.

Attach another length of ribbon to the back of the panel for hanging the door plate.

KEY for Angelina sequence			
	DMC	Colour	Stitches
✳	318	grey	55
✕	761	dark pink	257
U	762	light grey	410
O	819	pale pink	46
+	963	pink	602
•		white	70
	317	dark grey	backstitch

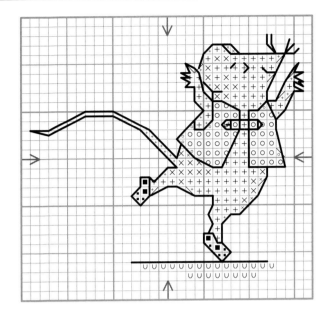

KEY for Henry		
DMC	Colour	Stitches
O 307	yellow	50
■ 317	grey	11
U 772	green	24
× 841	fawn	30
+ 842	mushroom	106

Backstitch

310	black	eye & mouth
317	grey	shoes, pin & ground
839	brown	other details

Congratulations Card

Henry hasn't quite learned the finer details of dance, but he tries hard. Here is a lovely card for a child who has achieved or simply made an attempt.

Materials: 14 x 14 cm of white Aida fabric with 14 thread groups per inch; 37.5 x 12.5 cm of cream card; double-sided tape; ribbon; DMC embroidery threads listed.

Stitch count: 26H x 30W

Directions: Stitch the design on the Aida. On one side of the cream card, lightly score two lines and fold, creating three even panels. Use a compass to pencil a 4 cm-radius circle in the centre panel and cut it out with a sharp knife. Apply double-sided tape on the inside of the window and place the stitched work so that it shows through. Tape down the left-hand panel. With the compass, emboss a circle 7 mm outside the window. Decorate with a ribbon.

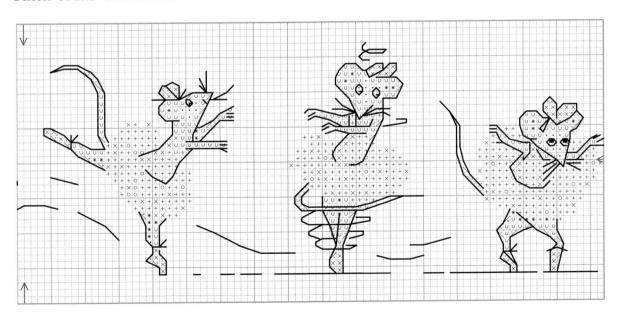

Apple
Tree
Farm

Apple Tree Farm

This chapter contains a whole cast of popular characters: the creatures who live at Apple Tree Farm. Farmyard Tales is a collection of delightful stories written by Heather Amery and illustrated by Stephen Cartwright. Each story has been written for children who are just beginning to read and recounts the adventures of Mrs Boot the farmer, her children Poppy and Sam, and their dog Rusty. The stories recreate the daily chores and activities of life on a farm (something of a mystery to city children) in a gentle and humorous way. A day for the Boot family is never dull—a lost piglet, a runaway tractor, a prize-winning donkey—there is always some excitement. The many animals are the real stars of the show, as Stephen Cartwright endows each one with distinctive and quirky characteristics. Duck, the hero of an earlier chapter in this book, makes a return appearance throughout. Audio taped readings and a press-out model farm bring these endearing tales very much to life.

Alphabet Sampler

This charming alphabet can be stitched as a complete sampler or as individual letters. There are no half-stitches in the designs, making them ideal for those just learning to cross-stitch.

Materials: 75 x 75 cm of white Aida fabric with 14 thread groups per inch; DMC embroidery threads listed.

Stitch count: 273H x 273W

Directions: Tack one thread across the Aida fabric and another from top to bottom, marking the centre of the fabric. Stitch the letter 'K' which is in the centre of the design, and then work out from there. The diagram below indicates how the charts fit together.

When all the letters are completed, add a red border one stitch wide around the whole design. Carefully press the finished work and have it professionally framed.

	p.105	p.106	p.107
	p.109	p.112	p.113

	KEY for alphabet sampler		
	DMC	Colour	Stitches
/	224	pink	40
◆	300	russet	377
∴	301	rust	291
■	310	black	176
▲	334	grey-blue	614
Z	407	fawn	541
✳	414	grey	761
→	415	light grey	477
H	436	light brown	112
↑	444	yellow	464
T	469	dark green	209
—	471	green	996
○	606	flame	477
⁒	647	grey-green	332
X	666	red	3310
<	677	straw	359
>	734	olive	237
N	740	orange	206
F	780	dark tan	262
4	782	light tan	138
＼	798	dark blue	274
●	839	mud	288
⊡	840	mushroom	391
+	945	flesh	239
I	950	peach	403
∩	972	gold	299
s	977	bronze	573
∪	3042	mauve	314
=	3072	silver	773
≠	3328	rose	188
·		white	389

Backstitch

407	fawn	arm & chin of F
414	grey	J, M, body of Z
839	mud	D, G, pig in P
310	black	other details

KEY for alphabet sampler

	DMC	Colour	Stitches
/	224	pink	40
◆	300	russet	377
∴	301	rust	291
■	310	black	176
▲	334	grey-blue	614
Z	407	fawn	541
✳	414	grey	761
→	415	light grey	477
H	436	light brown	112
↑	444	yellow	464
T	469	dark green	209
−	471	green	996
○	606	flame	477
∕	647	grey-green	332
×	666	red	3310
<	677	straw	359
>	734	olive	237
N	740	orange	206
F	780	dark tan	262
4	782	light tan	138
＼	798	dark blue	274
●	839	mud	288
⊡	840	mushroom	391
+	945	flesh	239
I	950	peach	403
∩	972	gold	299
s	977	bronze	573
∪	3042	mauve	314
=	3072	silver	773
≠	3328	rose	188
•		white	389

Backstitch

407	fawn	arm & chin of F
414	grey	J, M, body of Z
839	mud	D, G, pig in P
310	black	other details

The Farm Alphabet

A is for apple tree
B is for barn
C is for chicken
D is for dog
E is for eggs
F is for farmer
G is for goat
H is for horse
I is for ivy
J is for jumper
K is for kitten
L is for lamb
M is for mouse
N is for nest
O is for owl
P is for pig
Q is for quack
R is for rabbits
S is for scarecrow
T is for tractor
U is for umbrella
V is for vegetables
W is for wheelbarrow
X is for ten apples
Y is for yellow
Z is for sleeping soundly.

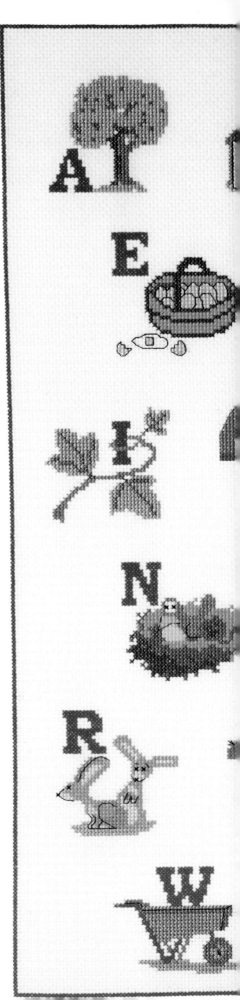

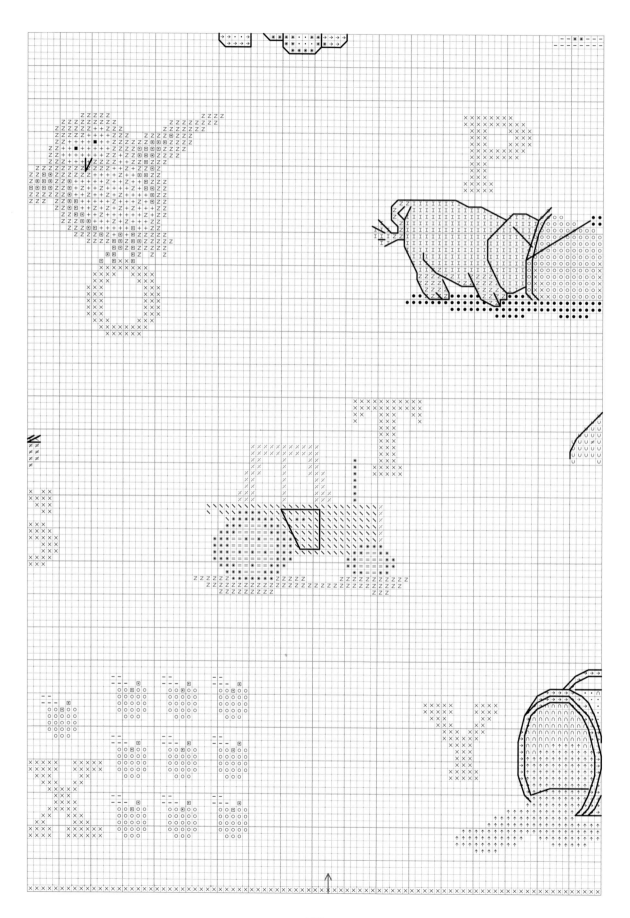

Rupert

This young bear lives in the village of Nutwood, which is somewhere in England, with his parents, Mr and Mrs Bear. Rupert, instantly recognisable in his jolly red jumper, yellow checked trousers and scarf, has a keen interest in solving life's mysteries, and mysteries are in great supply in Nutwood. Together with his friends, Rupert finds himself involved in extraordinary adventures, often travelling through time and space, but always returning home in time for tea. He first appeared in the Daily Express in 1920 and proved such an appealing character that Rupert Annuals were soon published. He is now the star of a delightful animated television series and over fifty million of his books have been sold worldwide.

Rupert, always the model of good manners, would doubtless be modestly surprised by his enduring success.

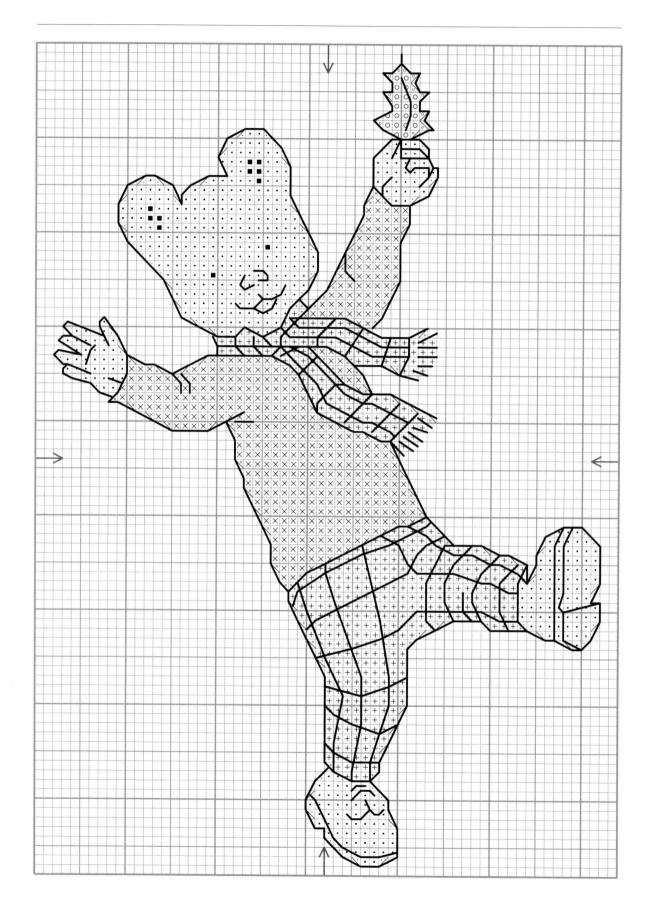

Christmas Stocking

KEY for Rupert with leaf			
	DMC	Colour	Stitches
■	310	black	11
+	444	yellow	511
✕	666	red	481
○	905	green	31
·		white	544
	310	black	backstitch

Rupert's colours make him an ideal subject for Christmas. This dashing stocking could also be personalised with a child's name.

Materials: 40 x 45 cm of green Aida fabric with 14 thread groups per inch; red bias binding; DMC embroidery threads listed.

Stitch count: 86H x 60W

Directions: Enlarge the pattern for the stocking by 250%, using a photocopying machine or by rescaling the pattern (on the left). Fold the Aida fabric in two and pin the pattern on top, then cut out the shape to give you two matching pieces.

Stitch the design in the lower section of one piece (as shown in the picture on page 115). Carefully press the finished work.

Lay the two sections of stocking together with the design facing up and sew red bias binding around the sides and foot of the stocking. Finish the opening with another piece of bias binding. Add a hanging loop made from bias binding if desired.

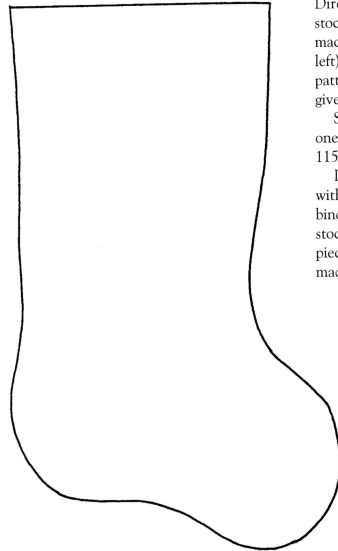

Patch

A patch can be sewn onto a variety of objects, such as the backpack on the opposite page.

Materials: 15 x 15 cm white Aida fabric
with 18 thread groups per inch;
15 x 15 cm white backing cloth;
DMC embroidery threads listed.

Stitch count: 58H x 61W

Directions: Stitch the design on Aida.
Use a compass to draw a pencil circle around
the design. Lay the Aida, design face up, on
backing cloth. Zigzag with 4 mm stitches

	KEY for Rupert in his car		
	DMC	Colour	Stitches
■	310	black	6
−	415	light grey	283
O	444	yellow	216
X	471	green	790
U	647	dark grey	183
+	666	red	207
•		white	356
	310	black	backstitch

around the circle in red thread, using the
pencil line as the outside edge. Trim along
the outside of the zigzags. Zigzag again to
create a well-bound edge.

Photo Frame

This cheery frame for a child's favourite photograph is pictured on page 119. Adjust the size of the window to suit your photograph.

Materials: 35 x 28 cm of white Aida fabric with 14 thread groups per inch; 28 x 22 cm of sturdy white card; double-sided tape; DMC embroidery threads listed.

Stitch count: 84H x 75W + photo area

Directions: Sew a line of tacking to mark a rectangle 13 cm high and 9 cm wide in the centre of the Aida fabric. This will be the photograph area (adjust the size if desired). Stitch the design so that the dashed lines match the corners of your tacking. Press the finished work. Cut a window measuring 11 x 7 cm in the centre, 1 cm in from each tacking line. Snip towards each tacked corner to form a mitre.

Cut a window, 13 x 9 cm, in the card. Lay the card mount on the back of the stitched design and place strips of double-sided tape around the window. Turn the mitred edges over and press them onto the tape. Turn the outside edges of the fabric over and secure with more tape. Remove the tacking stitches. Add a colourful frame if desired.

KEY for Rupert with kite			
	DMC	*Colour*	*Stitches*
■	310	black	5
○	444	yellow	423
✕	666	red	443
+	701	green	205
•		white	249
	310	black	backstitch

Rupert Character ™ & © 1995 Express Newspapers plc. All rights reserved.

Pillowcase

Rupert, in his frightfully English pyjamas, has been stitched over waste canvas onto a pillowcase of fine cotton fabric.

Materials: 15 x 15 cm of waste canvas with 14 thread groups per inch; a white cotton pillowcase; DMC embroidery threads listed.

Stitch count: 62H x 57W

Directions: Position the waste canvas in the top-right of the pillowcase, near the opening. Tack around the edges and also diagonally so that the canvas is securely attached to one layer of the pillowcase.

Stitch the design, then remove tacking threads. Dampen the canvas with a cloth and carefully pull out the strands.

KEY for Rupert on the moon			
	DMC	Colour	Stitches
■	310	black	7
U	321	red	40
\	743	yellow	849
O	794	blue	353
•		white	163

Backstitch

	white	pyjama stripes
310	black	other details

These alphabets and numbers can be used to personalise many projects in this book.

Below: chart for Cloth Book
Stitch each animal name in the
centre of a fabric 'page'.

Above: pattern for the
Feeding Bib (page 45)

Acknowledgements

The charts in this book were created with StitchCraft, a Windows-based software program for designing counted charts. For information on this program, please contact Crafted Software at:
UK: PO Box 166, Middlesbrough, Cleveland TS5 8YF, Telephone & Fax: 01642 598010
Australia: PO Box 78, Wentworth Falls NSW 2782, Telephone: 61 47 573136 Fax: 61 47 573337

Thanks to Yoram Gross for permission to include Blinky Bill designs.
Blinky Bill © Angus & Robertson 1939. Licensed by Gaffneys.

Beatrix Potter ™ © Frederick Warne & Co 1995.

Babar and the distinctive likeness thereof are trademarks of Laurent de Brunhoff and are used with his permission, and courtesy of Nelvana Limited and The Clifford Ross Company, Ltd. Copyright © Laurent de Brunhoff. All Rights Reserved.

Spot ™ © Eric Hill/Salspot, 1995.

Miffy and other illustrations by Dick Bruna, © Mercis b.v.

Paddington Bear ™ © Paddington and Company Ltd 1995. Licensed by Copyrights.

Duck designs and illustrations are taken from the *Find the Duck* and *Duck and his Friends* illustrated by Stephen Cartwright and published by Usborne Publishing Ltd.

Angelina books are published by ABC, The All Children's Company Limited.

Apple Tree Farm designs and illustrations are taken from the *Usborne Farmyard Tales* illustrated by Stephen Cartwright and published by Usborne Publishing Ltd.

Licensed by NELVANA
TM & © Express Newspapers p.l.c.

Special thanks to those who helped to stitch the designs: Maryse Pedersen, Judy Chambers, Mary Kuitert, Jennifer Kuitert and Joanna Simpson.

Thanks, too, to Aileen Curie, Liz Farquharson and Melody Wickham from Copyrights and Catherine Walsh from Gaffneys who rescued this project on several occasions.

The author is also grateful to:
DMC for fabrics and embroidery threads used throughout
Shearers of Gordon for books used in various photographs
A Fine Line of Mosman for the suitcase on page 63
Summer Hill Arts & Crafts for framing
Bloch in the Strand Arcade of Sydney for ballet items on pages 94 and 98

Index